PRESSURE GROUPS AND THE
PERMISSIVE SOCIETY

PEOPLE, PLANS AND PROBLEMS SERIES

General editor: Professor J. B. Mays
Department of Sociology
University of Liverpool

Others in the series

PRESSURE GROUPS AND THE PERMISSIVE SOCIETY

BRIDGET PYM
BA, Lecturer in Sociology,
Sheffield University

DAVID & CHARLES   *Newton Abbot*

0 7153 6451 0

JN
329
P7
P93
3012247

Set in 11/13 point Plantin
and printed in Great Britain
by W J Holman Limited Dawlish Devon
for David & Charles (Holdings) Limited
South Devon House Newton Abbot Devon

Contents

Foreword

'And will it have been worth it after all?'

This book is about pressure groups. It investigates how much they are able to achieve in the way of influencing governments to make laws. It is aimed at the general reader, but may also have something to offer the student.

Maybe no one should enjoy this book, for it is cudgelled out of the blood, sweat and tears of one among hundreds struggling to survive in an academic rat race. To this end I have exploited and been served by many, ranging, I suppose, from Suzanne Backhouse, who inadvertently gave me the idea to the bookseller's assistant who sells you this copy. In between come the University of Sheffield, the Nuffield Foundation, the Association of British Directories, the representatives of the various pressure groups who gave so generously of their time and facilities, MPs and peers, the patient typists and research assistants, agents, publishers and editor, the people who ferried me on buses and trains to do the interviews and friends who lent me things, read bits and talked to me. My hands reach out. But next time—make the revolution!

7

1 *The Role of Pressure Groups*

Who makes Britain's laws, Parliament or people? In this book we shall see how pressure groups struggle to change or defend the law, scrutinise the reasons for their successes or failures and make some predictions for the future. Our starting point is the crop of controversial laws that caused journalists of the late 1960s to write of Britain as the permissive society.

The general election of 1964 brought to power a Labour administration, the first for 13 years. Perceiving the country to be in the throes of inflation and on the verge of bankruptcy, it turned for help to those international financiers, the 'Gnomes of Zurich', an act which seemingly precluded major structural reforms of British society. Yet, while Conservatives breathed a sigh of relief and constitutional radicals were reduced to cynicism, significant social changes were in fact taking place.

These did not start suddenly in 1964. Signs of change were evident from the early 1960s, beginning arbitrarily with the publication of the hitherto banned D. H. Lawrence novel, *Lady Chatterley's Lover*, in 1960, and continuing with the violent demonstration against Britain's nuclear defence policy, which in 1961 set a new trend in political activism at the same time as the satirical television programme *TW3* attacked establishment figures and values in a way not formerly encountered

by the Saturday night viewer. In 1963, as the Bishop of Wool-
wich's radical bestseller *Honest to God* challenged orthodox
theology, the Profumo scandal, involving a government minister and a call-girl, and the revelations of brutality in the
Sheffield police force undermined the credibility of authority
figures here below; and by 1964 the increasing boldness of the
mass media in their treatment of sex and violence was sufficient to engender the 'Clean-up TV' campaign. During the
1960s violence in America—on the campuses, in the ghettos,
on the streets—was reflected to a lesser, but in context no less
startling, degree in the major cities of Britain. This became the
era of swinging London, the mini-skirt, the 'underground' and
the drug problem, the whole played out against a mounting
crescendo of pop music as the semi-respectable Beatles yielded
to the aggressive sexuality of the Rolling Stones. This com-
pounding of protest, pop music and sex is perhaps false, since
the origins and purposes of each thread were rather different.
Yet collectively they shattered the once firm, well founded code
of civil conduct which, despite erosions, had dominated Britain
for over 40 years. The Labour government 1964–70 supported
and even initiated changes, by suspending captial punishment
for a 5 year period, widening the grounds for legal abortion,
abolishing penalties for certain homosexual acts, extending
the grounds for divorce and abolishing theatre censorship.

Although many changes take place in society without legal
battles, law has a special significance, for it lays practical and
psychological constraints on our buying and selling, drinking
and driving, marrying and burying—in fact, overtly or covertly
on almost every area of life. It is therefore important to know
who makes the law, and how far its subjects are able to influence the legislative process.

Few people believe it either feasible or desirable for the
mass of the population to be directly involved in lawmaking.
The British system is for them to elect representatives—an

elite, in fact. But once it is accepted that lawmaking is the province of elites, significant questions arise as to the relationship of these elites to the mass. Clearly an elite acting only in its own interests is a major threat to democracy. Descriptive models of the British political system comfortingly see the policy-making process as one of complex exchanges between electorate, constituency parties, parliamentary parties, civil service, cabinet and prime minister.[1] The government (ie ministers) and the civil service are generally seen as the real centres of power, but particular policies emerge through an interweaving of party doctrine, electoral considerations, domestic pressures, international exigencies and personal idiosyncracies. According to this model particular individuals in strategic positions—ministers, party advisers, union leaders—may be able to make significant interventions, but the contribution of the man on the Clapham omnibus seems to get lost in the miasma of interactions. One avenue by which the loaded Clapham omnibus supposedly approaches the seat of government is via the activities of pressure groups.

By pressure groups we mean subsections of the population organised on the basis of fairly specific common interests or attitudes, and aiming to influence government. There is a danger that by concentrating our attention on such groups we may make them seem more important than they are, for there are all sorts of elements in the political situation, ranging through foreign governments and constituency parties to the psychological problems of MPs. Among these, pressure groups are correctly seen to be of only limited significance.

An example of how some people perhaps overestimate the role of groups is to be found in the book by Mrs Mary Whitehouse, a staunch opponent of the trend towards permissiveness and defender of established standards through the Clean-up TV campaign and later the evangelical Festival of Light movement. She laid the blame for permissive legislation at the door of the radical pressure groups thus :

> Permissive reforms are now being pushed through Parliament one by one. Although they command support from vocal minorities it would be a mistake to believe they represent the wish of the majority of ordinary people. And it is becoming more and more clear that the motivating group behind them are the British Humanist Association, the National Secular Society, the Homosexual Law Reform Society and the Abortion Law Reform Society.[2]

Although she asserts the right of groups to work for these things if they choose, Mrs Whitehouse's hostile tone casts doubts on the legitimacy of pressure-group operations in the process of lawmaking.

Yet many political writers on both sides of the Atlantic have seen pressure groups as significant and positive contributors to the process of democracy. They argue that in modern society there are many decisions on the conduct of life, distribution of resources, etc, which have to be taken at a national level, and, mass participation being impossible, the basic means of decision-making in societies with democratic pretensions is through representatives elected on broad party platforms and assuming between elections responsibility for decision-taking in what theoretically is the national interest. At the same time, to ensure that these representatives do not deliberate as Olympians in isolation from the needs and wishes of the populace, a steady flow of information between governing and governed is essential, and to this end pressure groups organised to represent sectional interests as between labour and capital or interests on particular issues such as conservation or simplified spelling are essential. How many of us belong to unions, professional associations, welfare trusts, amenity societies and consumer groups in the vague expectation that, among other things, they will be ready to defend our interests when the legislature neglects or impinges on them. Constituency parties, local authorities, even foreign governments are, in some formulations, regarded as pressure groups on government. In theory, pressure groups keep governments in touch with popular feeling and ply them with expert advice on the desirability or otherwise of changes. Participation guarantees the health of the body politic.

Of course there will be conflicts of interest as between employers and employed, car users and country dwellers, and, as we have already intimated, there are a multiplicity of other forces at work besides those of identifiably organised interest groups; but in theory the legislature provides a forum where competing contestants can canvass support. Legislators are usually seen as standing at the focal point of interactions, striving to reconcile different interests in pursuit of a national good, consonant with their basic conservative or socialist assumptions. Groups are at least able to enter the arena, and justice and good sense generally prevail, in that the policies adopted tend to reflect the balance of interests in society while safeguarding the needs of minorities.

Groups thus sustain democracy. Admittedly few if any of them are mass organisations in the sense of being actively controlled by the mass of their members. Most likely they are controlled by elites, some of whom, such as captains of industry or religious leaders, are of sufficient importance in national life to be bracketed with the governmental elite itself. Others, like cyclists or vegetarians, though elitist in the sense of being run by a minority of activists, are scarcely elites in that sense, and are more generally referred to simply as pressure groups. In what follows we shall normally use the expression 'pressure groups' to embrace both types.

Many of our assumptions about groups in Britain stem from generalised accounts written some 15 years ago when the subject suddenly became fashionable.[3] The picture then presented, substantially endorsed by later authors,[4] sees groups as contributing at most stages of the legislative and administrative process. In areas like industry or education, for example, where government policies are not implemented by coercion, but depend on the daily activities of employers, unions and teachers, the views of groups are particularly important because success depends on their co-operation and their technical advice is often a vital component in policy-making. Such groups, it was said, are constantly consulted by governments. By contrast small reformist groups like the abortion law reformers or the anti-vivisectionists are not. The reasons for this are not always clearly brought out. Stewart says:

> The cause group represents only a point of view about the way in which the government and parliament should act, in many cases a point of view very far from being generally accepted. But even when its viewpoint is accepted the group cannot expect to be automatically consulted. *It is not necessary to the conduct of affairs.*

Walkland more helpfully suggests that the 'cause' groups lack political and economic sanctions.[5]

Some groups, then, are more effective than others, but all the commentators emphasise that the role of even the most prominent groups is one of influence rather than power. Real power lies with the government and its departments. Groups can do little against a hostile government, and even with a sympathetic one can only cooperate as juniors. Groups are contained by the wisdom of the political guardians.

In crude summary, groups do intervene, those socially significant more effectively than others, but all the same governments retain control.

Thus presented, the picture contains much that is appealing to the democratic eye. Only Finer seems to betray serious reservations about the role of groups, yet there is another body of authors who, by highlighting arguments that are at best latent in these works, imply that group activity, far from being a major channel of democratic influence for the ordinary man, generally operates to the advantage of the already powerful.[6] It is not a leveller, it is a fraud. They argue firstly that while some groups do participate, many important ones do not; secondly, that among those groups which compete in the political arena some enjoy systematic and unfair advantages in the competition; and thirdly, following therefrom, that the legislators, far from being the moral neutrals implied by the above theory, tend to favour certain groups over others. Thus in their view, group representation at best works only in a limited fashion, and even where it does operate, it fails to do so fairly and openly.

To elaborate: every government influences taxation and retail prices, yet taxpayers, housewives and other consumers are poorly organised, if at all. The pensioners, the sick and the poor tend to be difficult to mobilise, while persons whose activities are illegal (eg, homosexuals before 1967) have obvious difficulties in maintaining a legitimate organisation. There are all sorts of potential interest groups in our society that are not formally constituted and thus do not effectively compete in the political arena.

Again, even for those groups that have sufficient will, fortune and know-how to enter the competition, the outcome is biased, since groups are not equal competitors. In a 'good' world, competing points of view could be reconciled to mutual advantage, or perhaps the most meritorious case would triumph, but in the 'real' world people capitulate to demands because of what they hope to gain or fear to lose. I capitulate not because you are right but because you will punish me if I do not or reward me if I do. Your ability to punish or reward depends on your ability to give or withhold what I want—peace, affection, money—or on your ability to make life unpleasant for me. The victors in bargaining situations, therefore, are the parties that best control the resources and lives of their adversaries. Among pressure groups putting their claims before the government we would guess that the most successful would be those commanding resources such as expertise or investment capacity vital to a complex economy.

Groups start with unequal bargaining strength, therefore, and they are also unequal in terms of organisational effectiveness, quality of leadership and wealth (the key to effective propaganda), all of which are means to successful representation. In addition, some groups, like unions or employers' organisations, are comparatively respected and respectable, while others are dismissed as cranks. Groups whose aims are consonant with commonly held social values are more likely to be acceptable than groups with esoteric standpoints; but a further factor, which in a 'democratic' society enhances the legitimacy of a group, is its size and the extent to which it can be seen to be representative. A tiny group, purporting to stand for wide consumer interests, say, which cannot substantiate its claim to have their backing, will be ignored.

Even our first group of political writers, alive to differences between groups, drew up lists of attributes whose possession it was conjectured meant success or failure for pressure groups.[7] The critical school of thought represented in recent years by C. Wright Mills in America and Ralph Miliband in Britain, however, implies that the minor inequalities between particular unions, or between different moral-reform groups, pales into insignificance before the overriding divide between the superior endowment of the moneyed interest versus the rest. The most crucial differentiation is the crude division between employers and employed. Wealthy interests can afford to pay for superior propaganda, oratory and know-how. Their control over the wages and, hence, living standards of the employed gives them superiority in bargaining. Before the Industrial Revolution government control in Britain rested almost solely in the hands of the propertied class, and even after manhood suffrage was made universal it seems to Mills and Miliband that power remained largely in the hands of the rich. Business still dominates, both directly, in that legislators tend to be drawn from upper-class backgrounds, and also more subtly, in that the operations of any government, right or left, are circumscribed by the capitalist values of acquisition, competition and materialism. These values are so strongly entrenched that alternative values scarcely receive acknowledgement. Further and equally important, on any issue government policies will be subject to the control the moneyed class wields over technical resources, contracts and investment, without which few projects are possible in industrial society.

These criticisms stem from radicals who maintain that either pluralism (an equal competition of alternative interest groups) does not exist or that in so far as it does it is systematically biased in the interests of a minority. However, right wingers and democrats have their complaints, too. Mrs Whitehouse apparently did not fear domination by business interests so much as the disproportionate influence of small radical pressure groups, while among American commentators McConnell[8] has raised similar objections to group intervention, arguing that strong government is the only way to avoid the despotism of sectional interests. Who makes the law? That is the question. We have to discover whether ordinary people have, via the medium of pressure groups, a say in framing that law; whether all sections of the population participate equally; how the political elite copes with competing claims; and whether some groups can wield more influence than others in its decisions.

The dominance of economic interests on economic matters— the allocation of resources, taxation, employment policies, etc —follows obviously from the critical model. But does this mean that economic interests will dominate in other areas of life, such as education, religion or sexual morals? The sociologists who stress the necessary coherence of all aspects of social life will argue that in these spheres also the wishes of the economic overlords will be paramount, since they could not afford, and are in a position to prevent, society fostering, say, an educa-

B

tional system whose values might ultimately undermine the economic sector.

This problem is specially pertinent to what follows, for we shall focus particularly on recent changes in the law on moral issues. Our evidence is drawn from Hansard, from the minute books and papers of individual pressure groups and from questionnaires and interviews with the principals involved. Chapter 2 looks at the seemingly fruitless struggle of radical groups to effect changes in the law. Chapter 3 discusses the organisational characteristics of the radical and conservative groups. Our exploration into this subject began with the assumption that groups would prove to be important and that the main thing was to investigate why some groups were more successful than others. However, as research progressed, it appeared that we had overestimated the direct role of groups. On the whole decisions seemed to lie in the hands of government and MPs. Chapters 4 and 5 describe these findings in detail, with illustrations drawn from particular case histories. Chapter 5 begins by defining the role played by government, and then goes on to explore the less tangible problem of what influences act on our legislators. By Chapter 6 we feel we have reached a position in which we may match the pluralist model and its critics against our findings.

The first six chapters concentrate on a particular area of law-making—private members' bills on 'moral' issues. In Chapter 7 we consider how far our conclusions apply to other areas of legislation—economic matters like rents, control of monopolies or pollution. In Chapter 8 we look to the future, to ask whether past patterns will persist, or if groups could become more effective and whether or not it is desirable that they should be.

Notes to this chapter are on p169

2 *The Years of Victory for the In-groups*

The number and range of groups upon the British political scene is vast and various, ranging from massive multi-purpose groups like the Transport & General Workers Union to small groups set up to preserve some local beauty spot. No one knows how many there are. The ways in which they could be classified are manifold—occupational, recreational, and welfare; large and small; radical and reactionary; and all mixtures of all these—but the most important dividing line is between groups that are politically acceptable and groups that are not. Out-groups are out because they propagandise for unpopular causes or minority interests, or because they are judged unrepresentative of those they claim to speak for. In-groups, that is to say those readily and regularly admitted to consultations with government departments, may derive their legitimacy from their indispensability to the economy, because they speak for acceptable causes like animal or child welfare or because, like church groups, they have become over the years simply part of the British way of life. The differences in style and significance between the out-group and the in-group can be illustrated by contrasting the radical pressure groups seeking for moral reform and the church groups which for many years opposed them.

Groups have found a new role as government business has expanded from its former responsibilities for defence, foreign affairs and tariffs to include education, social services, economic policy, opera, railways, coal and aero-space.[1] The routine administration of these affairs constitutes the major preoccupation of government departments, and must be the major area for pressure-group activity. As regards the more eyecatching business of lawmaking, most of it is government-sponsored, and derives from party policy or from governmental reaction to current imperatives.[2] Details are formulated in Whitehall, with or without discussion with pressure groups, and once a bill is introduced into Parliament, its success is generally assured through the automatic support of the MPs of the majority party. To be involved in this process it is almost essential to be an in-group. Although most parliamentary time in Britain is consumed in government business under the direction of party leaders, small sections known as private members' time are also available for backbenchers to introduce legislation and debates on subjects of broadly their own choosing. Any pressure group whose cause is not sufficiently important or respectable to warrant inclusion in the government's own programme has to compete for this time. Matters of conscience, conventionally but surely arbitrarily defined as those with religious implications, have almost never formed part of a government's programme because no government feels it should compel people to vote against their conscientious beliefs. Thus bills on issues of sexual morality have had to compete with bills on foxhunting, hire purchase, simplified spelling and other useful but, by the government's definition, marginal reforms, for the tiny slice of time allowed for private members' legislation. The technical difficulties of the situation are aggravated by the fact that the groups desiring reform tend to be 'out' and are easily held at bay by those that are 'in'. The early years in the struggle for moral (or immoral) reforms demonstrates this perfectly.

To begin by recapturing the past, the years after World War I, normally associated with the rising star of the Labour Party in Parliament, with flappers and the General Strike, saw also a small but remarkable rise in the volume of protest against the long-established codes of morality. The blasphemies of the National Secular Society which had outraged all decent opinion for 50 years suddenly found an audience and a wider measure of active support. A splintering of the movement produced societies for reform of the laws on franchise, blasphemy, religious education, divorce, capital punishment, cremation and latterly abortion and euthanasia. All struggles involved a redefinition if not rejection of the accepted religious position. By the 1930s the battle was being won on some fronts—over franchise and cremation, for instance. The birth-control movement was making progress against heavy opposition from civic dignitaries and the medical profession, the divorce law was reformed and the divorce and illegitimacy rates appeared to be rising. However, from the perspective of 1972 it seems to most people that the British of the immediate pre- and post-war period were comparatively straitlaced.

As late as 1950 sociologist Geoffrey Gorer, in a study of the attitudes of the British people, came to the conclusion that their love of freedom and sensitivity to others were conjoined with sexual inhibition, a strong attachment to marriage and the family, and an inordinate level of self-discipline inculcated by stern child-rearing practices.[3] More instructive than the percentages is the revealing fact that in 1950 Gorer did not think it diplomatic to ask his sample whether they had had premarital intercourse, let alone with how many partners. Nor did he question them on frequency of intercourse within marriage, or on their attitudes to homosexuality. By the time of his follow-up study in 1969, all these questions were both askable and answerable.[4] Gorer's statistical evidence supports the popular prejudice that in the 1950s people were less likely to have had premarital intercourse and more likely to regret it if they had. Over half the population, compared to rather less than half today, were virgin at marriage, and a similarly high proportion disapproved of premarital sex. The young of 1950 were, according to Gorer, stricter in their avowed attitudes than the young of today, when most of the engaged couples apparently go to bed with each other. There was little explicit discussion of sexual matters, no four-letter words in print, no nudity in the cinema, less sex in advertising than today. Homosexuality, even now stigmatised, was even more strongly censured and more valiantly concealed in the immediate post-war years.

The whole morality was underpinned by the expectation of strict self-discipline. Doctor Spock's 'spare the rod' policy was not yet fashionable. Adults were credited with free will, with the capacity to choose between good and evil and with consequent responsibility for their actions. To err was to display moral weakness and to deserve punishment—a view resulting in censorious attitudes towards unmarried mothers, homosexuals and adulterers as well as to thieves, swindlers and murderers. That murderers, obviously the most culpable of all, deserve only to be executed, was and is the belief of all but a tiny minority of the population. Following Gorer's reasoning, the aggression we repress through our strict self-discipline is vented on the proven offender who has dared to convert our secret longings into reality.

Now it may be objected that this was only the surface morality, that there were proportionately almost as many divorces as today, possibly as many confirmed homosexuals, and thousands of love affairs, illegitimate births and illegal abortions.

However, notwithstanding breaches in the code among the young and the top and bottom sectors of society, the more elderly and the solid middle class (from professionals to skilled workers to whom respectability matters and to whom moral rectitude and self-control are no mean virtues) sustained the public code. It was barely questioned by either the church or the medical profession, most of whose members were recruited from the higher ranks of society. It was respected by the serious press and by the radio, and, importantly, by the law, which restricted divorce and punished homosexuality, abortion, suicide and, of course, murder.

The general dispositions to discipline and modesty were heightened by the discipline and endeavour of the war years and subsequently by the disciplines of the austerity period— of food rationing, clothing coupons and shortages, the 6 day working week and make-do-and-mend. Admittedly, as Britain moved into the 1950s, the evidence of the Sunday newspapers, Marilyn Monroe and Jane Russell, sexuality in advertising, and the genesis of youth culture and pop, all eroded the old system. But even then the force of public morality remained austere. In the mid-1950s Princess Margaret, 'mindful of the Church's teaching that Christian marriage is indissoluble' refused the hand of the divorced Group Captain Peter Townsend. Trials of homosexuals still referred discreetly to 'serious offences'. Four-letter words were still virtually unheard of in nice places. Private behaviour was restrictive compared with today, the public code even more so, and it was against this background that the radical pressure groups waged a struggle which lasted in some cases for over 30 years.[5] Why it took so long and why for so long groups apparently achieved so little we shall illustrate by means of two case studies, one on abortion and one on divorce. A further case history of capital punishment draws attention to some different considerations.

The Failure of Abortion Law Reform

In the 1930s the slow acceptance by the state of responsibility for the welfare of mothers and babies meant a growing awareness of the problems of poverty and childbirth. Many seriously concerned persons felt that the only moral answer was to improve knowledge of birth control, while others put their trust in social work and social welfare to provide for the pregnant mother and her unwanted child. So serious was the maternal morbidity and mortality problem that in 1935 the Ministry of Health, urged on by the National Council of Women, instituted an inquiry. Many hundreds of women could not wait for ministerial solutions to the hazards of childbearing and resorted to abortion. Abortions were, no doubt, performed in discreet nursing homes by qualified doctors on the daughters of the well-to-do, and also in back rooms on kitchen tables by well meaning ladies using unsterilised syringes and knitting needles. The law on abortion was highly restrictive, forbidding all 'unlawful attempts to procure a miscarriage' except where necessary to preserve the life of the mother; but this wording was not clear-cut enough to protect the doctor who had sympathies for a desperate client, and in 1935 Dr Aleck Bourne, who favoured greater clarification and some extension of the law, persuaded the British Medical Association to set up a committee to deliberate on the whole subject.

In the following year a group of women long associated with the birth-control campaign founded the Abortion Law Reform Association. They believed that no woman should bear a child against her will, be she an already overburdened mother or a professional woman for whom liberation from annual childbearing was a necessity if she were to play a full role in a man's world. Steps were quickly taken to form a supporting group of distinguished vice-presidents and a medico-legal council, which gave not only a semblance of respectability to an outrageous platform but also advice on how best to formulate the aims of the movement. The group swung into action with a conference and plans for pamphlets and did much proselytising through branch meetings of the Women's Cooperative Guild and Labour Party.

The strength of the opposition revealed itself when the BMA Council discussed the report of its committee.[6] The report itself was highly liberal—suggesting that the law be clarified and that the case be sympathetically considered for abortion on eugenic grounds and in cases of rape. Abortion for social reasons would, the committee thought, reduce the rate of criminal abortion, but its members agreed that non-medical reasons lay beyond a doctor's province. The meeting of the BMA General Council greeted the report with hostility. Most representatives protested that they had little or no doubt over how the existing law should be applied and expressed fears that legislation would lead to an unbridled surge of irresponsible demands for abortion.

Meanwhile the early activities of the Abortion Law Reform Association were largely propagandist. It worked through leaflets and meetings and, where possible, articles in the press; but few papers would handle its material. The group also had a meeting at the House of Commons with a handful of MPs known to be sympathetic to the birth-control lobby. The major initiative, however, did not lie in their hands and occurred in 1937, when the Ministry Committee on Maternal Morality recommended in its report that a special inquiry be mounted into abortion, both spontaneous and criminally induced.[7] The Ministry of Health responded by setting up a special inter-departmental committee on abortion, chaired by Sir Norman Birkett, QC. It cannot be claimed that ALRA was responsible for the instituting of this committee, though both it and the other women's organisations welcomed the initiative. It is always out of a confluence of forces that changes come.

The terms of reference of the Birkett Committee did not

encourage its members to consider liberal legislation—they were to enquire into 'the prevalence of abortion and the present law relating thereto, and to consider what steps can be taken by more effective enforcement of the law or otherwise to secure the reduction of maternal mortality and morbidity arising from this cause'. The members, announced on 24 May 1937, comprised mainly medical men, with the addition of two men of law, Lady Ruth Balfour of the National Council of Women, and Mrs Dorothy Thurtle, wife of the radical MP Ernest Thurtle and daughter of Labour leader George Lansbury. Preparation of a memo for Birkett was ALRA's most significant task of 1937.

The next year brought an unexpected liberalisation in case law when Dr Aleck Bourne, having procured an abortion for a 15 year old girl raped by guardsmen, handed himself over to the police for trial. Everything about the case was significant and sensational.[8] Dr Bourne's defence was that the operation was necessary to preserve the girl's psychological balance. The law allowed abortion to 'preserve the life of the mother', and in a summing-up which was to remain the major landmark for nearly 30 years, Mr Justice Macnaghten argued that 'if the doctor is of the opinion . . . that the probable consequences of the continuation of pregnancy would indeed make the woman a physical wreck, or a mental wreck, then he operates . . . for the purpose only of preserving the life of the mother'. Bourne was acquitted, and henceforward it was established that the concept of preserving the life of the mother included wider circumstances than those of the immediate threat of her death, and also that mental as well as physical health was a relevant consideration. Bourne was one of the circle of people who formed the Abortion Law Reform Association, but his trial was in no sense engineered by ALRA, which continued its programme much as before, addressing about fifty meetings during the year and producing new pamphlets. Membership now stood at 292, plus sixty-nine affiliated groups. In the early years, then, though ALRA contributed to an awakening climate, the significant steps towards reform came mainly from other quarters.

Early in June 1939 the Birkett Committee published its report.[9] The select committee and the royal commission are theoretically democratic institutions. Commissioners are selected by the relevant ministry on the basis of their dispassionate interest in the subject. Groups and individuals are invited to submit memoranda and give oral evidence. A great many do so and thus feed their ideas into the great complex of ministerial policy-making. Around twenty-seven organisations submitted evidence to the Birkett Committee, but as the evidence has not been published, one can only make inferences as to the line different witnesses may have taken.

The largest body of evidence came from groups likely to have been conservative—the Union of Catholic Mothers, the British Medical Association, the Westminster Catholic Federation, the Midland Catholic Medical Society, the British (later Royal) College of Obstetricians and Gynaecologists, the Mothers Union. There were 'expert' witnesses from the Institute of Animal Genetics and the Pharmaceutical Society, and evidence from a number of groups whose position one cannot reliably assess, like the Modern Churchman's Union, the National Birth Control Association, the Metropolitan Police, the Family Endowment Society and the Public Health Officers Association. The only groups likely to have pleaded for easier abortion were the Abortion Law Reform Association, the Eugenics Society, the Society for the Provision of Birth Control Clinics, the North-Western Federation of Societies for Equal Citizenship, the East Midlands Working Women's Association and possibly the National Council of Women.

In reading the Birkett report one is vividly reminded of the stricter morality of bygone years. In those days contraception was morally suspect. The Birkett Committee considered whether wider instruction in the use of contraceptives might solve the abortion problem. It wrote: 'Among those practitioners prepared to advise their patients on it, many, we gathered, regard it as their duty to impart advice only when birth control is necessary on strictly medical grounds.' If contraception was thus strangulated, what hope was there for abortion? The commissioners agreed that the existing legal position, the Bourne judgment nothwithstanding, was not crystal clear, and they recommended that it be clarified but not extended. They explicitly rejected the demand of the Abortion Law Reform Association for what amounted to abortion on request as being 'contrary to religious and ethical teaching, and to the fundamental principles on which society is based, [which] . . . if given effect . . . would have serious consequences'. They examined the case for abortion on eugenic grounds for girls under 16 ('a direct temptation to loose conduct'), for cases of incest and rape and rejected them all, though they were sympathetic over the latter.

Their more positive proposals aimed (1) at alerting women to the dangers of abortion and stamping out the menace of the back-street abortionist by increased vigilance by doctors and police, and (2) at attacking the root cause of the demand for abortion, which was thought to be largely economic. Some members of the committee recommended more extensive contraceptive advice, but here Lady Balfour and Watts Eden expressed reservations. Other suggestions were for family allowances to counter poverty. A more charitable attitude towards unmarried mothers and better maternity services were also enjoined. Mrs Dorothy Thurtle issued a minority report expressing doubt about the degree of risk entailed in the operation and pleading for abortion to be made lawful for girls under 16, in cases of rape, and for eugenic reasons.

The committee had accepted the basic position of the

Catholic witnesses and the BMA rather than those of the radical groups. Their remedies were in the best humanitarian traditions of re-education and improved welfare services. The adverse committee report is a feature of the histories of capital punishment and divorce law reforms as well as abortion reform. It validates delay for the government that is indecisive or hostile to reform, and signifies a victory for the conservative pressure groups. For the time being all hope of reform disappeared and the outbreak of war eclipsed all other efforts.

The Labour Government which came to power after World War II undertook a massive programme of economic reform, nationalising many basic industries. The leaders of ALRA sounded out their small band of supporters in Parliament, but these counselled that not only would the heavy and important Labour programme crowd out such a subject as abortion reform but that it was too controversial to stand any hope of early success. Abortion as a 'moral' matter would in any case have to be raised during private members' time, which had been rescinded during the war years and was not restored until 1949. Furthermore, ALRA's leaders were now ageing and in poor health, and in face of all these obstacles the Association's activities flagged.

In 1948-9 the organisation gained two new and significant recruits in Glanville Williams, Reader in Jurisprudence (later Professor) at London University, and Dr Eustace Chesser. The latter wrote a pamphlet which was circulated during 1950 and 1951 to some 39,000 doctors, and to birth-control clinics, citizens' advice bureaux and other likely places. This publication produced so many appeals from women wanting abortions that the Association published a further leaflet, the *Enquirers Leaflet*, giving guidance on the state of the existing law.

In 1952, with the Conservatives back in power, the Association turned once more to Parliament. Private members' time is always in great demand, and MPs aiming to introduce bills have to draw lots for it. In 1952 ALRA was fortunate in that one of its supporters, rationalist Joseph Reeves, won a place and agreed to introduce an abortion Bill. An MP willing to introduce a Bill is a first step for a group, but only a small one —although twenty or so members may win time in the ballot, only the top half dozen have any real hope that their Bill will be enacted. Reeves had won only a lowly place, and his Bill shared the fate of many. According to convention the first debate on any Bill must be of sufficient length to permit a full airing of views, otherwise no vote can be taken, and without a vote the Bill cannot proceed to its next stage. It is not un-common for opponents of a Bill to prolong debates on earlier bills so that insufficient time remains for a Bill they dislike. This tactic can be successfully employed by just a handful of not particularly representative MPs, and so it is easier for small groups to obstruct than to engage in legislation. ALRA's biographers, Simms and Hindell, suggest that such tactics were employed against Reeves' Bill.[10] It came up in February 1953, but time ran out almost before he had begun to speak, and so his Bill was lost.[11]

Even if it had not been 'talked out' the Bill would probably not have secured a majority vote. Reeves was an outspoken and long-standing champion of unpopular causes. He claimed the support of a useful little band of MPs—including Douglas Houghton, husband of one of the ALRA Committee, and Kenneth Robinson, both of whom were to assume office in the 1964 Labour government—but probably most MPs were at best uncommitted and some, particularly the Roman Catholics, openly hostile. Outside Parliament, too, this rather mild Bill, which sought only to codify the Bourne judgment, provoked instant opposition in speeches from Roman Catholic dignitaries.

Later in 1953 Lord Amulree introduced an abortion Bill

into the House of Lords, but this made no progress after the failure of the sponsor to accede to the Association's pressure for 'social abortions' put the project in jeopardy.[12] Groups are always dependent on the goodwill of MPs and peers.

For a couple of years after these setbacks the Association seems to have slackened its efforts. There were changes in the composition of the executive as founder members retired or died and new people took over. At one stage Mrs Thurtle, the dissenting member of the Birkett Committee, became chairman. For all the changes, however, the nature of the group remained much the same—membership was around 200 and expenses less than £50 pa. The programme of activities continued as before, with executive members addressing the occasional meeting and writing letters and articles, but the main activity was discussion of a new Bill prepared by Glanville Williams and the drafting of a pamphlet that would help commend it to MPs. Some bodies were more progressive than others: for instance, in 1955 the Magistrates Association called for reform, but the radio programme 'Woman's Hour' refused to feature the subject. The parliamentary climate, too, was hostile, for in July 1955, when Kenneth Robinson asked in a private member's question whether it was not time for reform, the Home Secretary replied in the negative,[13] and in January of the following year, when Robinson again pressed the point, he was told that there there was 'no hope of legislation on this controversial subject'.[14]

However, the years 1957-60 saw ALRA trying nearly every channel of approach open to a pressure group working on Parliament. Each channel was blocked, but the Association's experience warrants a detailed exposition. Early in 1957 it tried to persuade selected MPs and peers to introduce a Bill, but by June it had met nothing but refusals and, somewhat disgruntled at its parliamentary supporters' caution, boldly talked of getting the government itself to take up the cause. But the government, in answer to letters and questions, saw no practical need for legislation now that improved health services had obviated the problems of the 1930s.

Undeterred by these setbacks, ALRA in 1958 set Glanville Williams to work on an ambitious Bill which included legalising abortion in cases of rape, and for eugenic and social reasons. A deputation of MPs sympathetic to the Bill was received cordially by the Home Secretary, but was given no promise of support. The topic was by now more freely discussed than hitherto. The Church of England and the BMA saw fit to reaffirm their opposition, but the mass media, if not always sympathetic, were at least giving the subject an airing. It is hard to realise now how daring it was then to bring such matters into the family living room. In May 1959 the Home Office again told ALRA that there was no hope of legislation. In 1960 the Association once more approached selected MPs, but its efforts were all to no avail.

The period 1957-60 was, therefore, one of failure, but in the annual ballot for private members' time late in 1960, abortion reform was given another chance when Kenneth Robinson won a place and decided to chance his arm with an abortion Bill. The Commons, of course, had its band of MPs sympathetic to abortion law reform, but it is wrong to assume that ALRA worked in close liaison with them. The Association always felt itself to be a supplicant, and that MPs were reluctant to identify with what was still considered rather an *outré* pressure group. It was by now conditioned to defeat, and its efforts in support of Robinson were cautious, even conspiratorial. He did, however, adopt the Association's version of the Bill, and ALRA and other organisations, such as the Ethical Union, the Secular Society, and the Eugenics Society, asked their members to write to MPs urging them to vote for it. The effective opposition again came from Roman Catholics.

The Bill's fortunes were, however, really a foregone conclusion, since Robinson, like Reeves, had only secured a low place in the ballot. In the debate the Home Office spokesman said that those parts of the Bill that aimed to codify Bourne were unnecessary and those parts that extended the grounds for abortion were generally unworkable.[15] The Minister was spared further worry, for, as anticipated, the Bill was talked out.

We shall not pursue the fortunes of ALRA beyond this point now, for subsequently things became easier for the reformers, and they were in the end able to achieve a great deal (see Chapter 3). For a second illustration of the battle for reform we shall turn to the history of divorce law reform.

The Failure of Divorce Law Reform

The old divorce law laid down that marriage was a matter of concern to society, in that it was a family link entailing obligations ranging from political favours to care of the aged; it was a means of regulating the ownership and inheritance of property, of providing the domestic necessities of life for all classes and for women the setting for their basic role and purpose in life. These practical implications combined with the bonds of love and the religious mystery of births and deaths made marriage an institution of immense importance. To many the idea of dissolving a marriage was tantamount to dissolving the fabric of society itself, and, therefore, marriages could only be dissolved lawfully if one of the partners had done something to destroy the very basis of the relationship. A partner who committed a matrimonial offence (eg adultery) became the 'guilty' party and could be divorced by the 'innocent' party. The former was not ordinarily entitled to

C

seek divorce, and divorce by mutual consent was not possible. After a divorce a 'guilty' man would normally be expected to pay maintenance to his ex-wife.

In the post-war era it seemed to many that these legal formulations were out of touch with the facts of marriage and divorce, and also with justice. The law claimed only to relieve the innocent, but there were generally 'faults on both sides', and if both parties were culpable or if both agreed that the marriage should terminate (ie, divorce by consent), the law still refused them a divorce, implying that their behaviour was irresponsible. Further serious stresses arose in cases where an 'innocent' party refused for religious, financial or vindictive reasons to divorce a 'guilty' party who wanted to go free.

The huge backlog of pending divorce cases in the years after World War II concentrated attention on the frustrating nature of the proceedings and the inadequacies of the law. Many radicals went further, feeling that the law should be widened to allow divorce by consent—especially divorce instigated by the 'guilty' party after a suitable period of separate living—so that dead marriages should not be prolonged by zealous or jealous partners. The need for reform was probably most obvious to the radical lawyer, and so it is not surprising that it was a London solicitor, Robert Pollard, who in 1946 founded the Marriage Law Reform Society, recruiting his first supporters as the chairs were stacked up against the wall after a meeting of the Progressive League. The small, newly formed group decided after some argument to work for limited rather than fundamental changes.

The body of divorce law is vast, embracing not just grounds for divorce but also matters of procedure, maintenance, custody, judicial separation, etc, and much of it in 1946, in the reformers' view, was in need of revision. So complex was the issue that they felt the first stage should be a thorough investigation by a royal commission. One of the earliest actions of the new group, therefore, was to send a circular letter to all the other radical societies urging them to press the Lord Chancellor to establish such a Commission. This had no apparent effect, and since private members' time was not restored to Parliament until 1949, there was no possibility of legislation. The group's programme was nevertheless an energetic one of holding meetings and publishing pamphlets. It also submitted useful evidence to the Denning Committee, which had been established by the Labour government to suggest some technical reforms of divorce law procedure in the light of the existing pressure on the courts. Denning's report went so far as to advocate divorce proceedings by either party after 7 years' separation. Meanwhile the society gained support and its members formed semi-autonomous branches here and there in provincial cities.

The parliamentary session of 1948–9 was the first postwar session to make time available for private members' Bills, though the understanding was that these must be uncontroversial so as not to interfere with the government's general programme. The case of a divorced lady anxious to marry her ex-husband's brother, a union prohibited under the existing rules, aroused the interest of Lord Mancroft, who in 1948 introduced a Bill into the Lords designed to amend the table of prohibited relationships. From the episcopal benches the Archbishop of Canterbury opposed the Bill on the grounds that it would introduce an undesirable element into the relation between a man and his sister-in-law,[16] and ultimately the Lord Chancellor killed it on the grounds that it was too controversial for the present session. Similar reasoning was used to prevent divorce law reform in the lower house, where a small band of reformers, led by Marcus Lipton, was pressing for changes independently of the MLRS. Early in 1948 Mr Lipton in a parliamentary question asked whether the Government would follow the Denning Committee's suggestion and legislate for divorce at the petition of either spouse (ie, not just the 'guilty' party), after 7 years' separation.[17] The Attorney General was noncommittal.

Lipton, of course, continued to work for reforms, and in the 1948-9 session two bills coming before the lower house were the occasion for a link-up between the parliamentary group and the MLRS. On the Married Women's Maintenance Bill the MLRS suggested some amendments that were accepted by the Bill's sponsors. The Society's members were alerted to write to MPs in support, but the clause containing the amendments met with some opposition from the judiciary, was labelled 'controversial' and was dropped.[18] The second Bill, the innocent-sounding Law Reform Bill, which was introduced to amend technical anomalies in matrimonial law, provoked dramatic scenes in the summer of 1949 when Mr Lipton, attempting to force some action on the question of divorce by either party after 7 years' separation, sought to introduce such a clause into the Bill.[19] The MLRS smartly organised a small supporting petition (4,000 signatures) and Mr Lipton's gesture attracted widespread support from sufferers all over the country. However, this clause, too, was ruled 'controversial', a decision which confirmed the MLRS's belief that only after a Royal Commission would substantial changes in the law be achieved. On 20 July Mr Lipton asked the Prime Minister, Mr Attlee, whether he would support such a commission and was met with a flat 'No sir'.[20] The post-war Labour government was admittedly preoccupied by an extremely heavy programme of significant legislation, but in addition its leaders, conditioned by an older brand of society tempered with Nonconformity, were never very interested in issues like abortion and divorce reform.

In the following months the MLRS continued to grow. More branches were formed and conferences held. The executive continued to urge the need for a Royal Commission in the press and on prospective MPs in the 1950 election, and in the new Labour government 100 MPs led by Marcus Lipton signed a motion to that end—but no official concessions were forthcoming. In the Lords on 23 November 1950 Lord Mancroft initiated a debate calling for a Royal Commission, and cited various points at which matrimonial law was confused and unjust.[21] Opposition came from various sides for different reasons: the Archbishop of York opposed any move to make divorce easier; the Lord Chancellor said it would be sensible to await the results of the new legal-aid scheme, and denied vehemently that the existing law on collusion was so abused as to be worthless.

In the ballot for private members' time late in 1950 a high place was secured by Mrs Eirene White, who was enjoined by Marcus Lipton to put forward a radical divorce law reform Bill, the restriction to uncontroversial matters in such bills having now been lifted. Mrs White decided to present a straightforward Bill on the issue of divorce after 7 years' separation, and the MLRS organised a supportive campaign of meetings, leaflets and press articles, and prompted a fierce onslaught on MPs' mailbags by its members. Efforts by Lipton and Mrs White to secure voting support revealed that the Bill was not popular with either party, but they still managed to gather a skilful band of independently minded enthusiasts, and, as it turned out, their organisation caught their opponents by surprise.[22] Towards the end of the second reading debate the Attorney General, in a calculated move, offered to institute a Royal Commission in return for the withdrawal of the Bill. This offer was ultimately accepted, for although the measure secured a large majority at the end of its second reading, its sponsors inclined to see this as a freak result and felt that so controversial a Bill would undoubtedly be blocked later in its passage, or would be killed by the end of the Parliament.

The resulting Royal Commission on Marriage and Divorce received over 1,000 memoranda and letters, and heard witnesses for some forty-one days.[23] Much of the debate was over minor technical matters. The central issues were firstly whether it was feasible to introduce divorce by consent (ie, by agreement of parties even though no matrimonial offences like adultery or cruelty had been committed) and secondly whether divorce proceedings might after all be instigated by the 'guilty' party. On these issues the witnesses can be divided into two camps. On the conservative side were all the church groups (except the Free Church Federal Council) plus the Bar Council and the various associations of the teaching profession. The radical side was largely made up of small non-establishment groups—the Marriage Law Reform Society, the Ethical Union, the Progressive League, the Fabian Society, the Haldane Society (a legal group), the Divorce Law Reform Union and the Women's Cooperative Guild. Mrs White, Lord Mancroft and Prof L. C. B. Gower were notable witnesses for the radical cause, and Jocelyn Simon, QC, and Lord Merriman, the President of the Probate, Divorce and Admiralty Division of the High Court, gave evidence against.

The radical groups all supported divorce after 7 years' separation at the instigation of the guilty party on the grounds that such marriages were obviously finished and resulted in illicit but permanent unions, illegitimate children, and defiance of maintenance orders. The MLRS supported these arguments with a rather unreliable survey of its members, but this was at least more evidence than was adduced by the conservatives, whose case rested on unsubstantiated arguments. Strong opposition came from the Bar Council, the Mothers Union, the Church of England, the Catholic Union and others, on the grounds that no person should be allowed to take advantage of his own wrongdoing and that no innocent spouse should be divorced against her will, especially as deserted wives would thus undeservedly lose their pension rights, these being tied up with their husbands' insurance contributions. Radicals and conservatives naturally took opposite sides on the issue of divorce by consent.

Many bodies pronounced on the general effects of divorce, some seeing it as a threat to all that was fine and decent in society. Everyone stressed the fundamental importance of marriage and the family, a view cogently and finely expressed in the Church of England memoranda:

> The Church believes that the person is the direct object of God's love, and that the family is the unit of society with which each person is intended to grow and develop to maturity. If society as a whole is to be healthy and stable, the family unit must be maintained in its entirety.[24]

Some groups felt that easier divorce prompted divorce-mindedness. The Methodist memorandum argued that it encouraged people to run away from their problems; while that of the Marriage Guidance Council stated categorically that easier divorce lessened respect for marriage, though on being questioned on this point the representatives could bring forward no evidence.

Much argument revolved round the effects of divorce on children. The Church of England and the Mothers Union argued that there was abundant evidence, from the experience of teachers and magistrates, that divorce led to delinquency and maladjustment among children of divorced parents. The representatives of the Mothers Union and the Baptist Union thought an unhappy home was better than no home. The Association of Headmistresses and the National Union of Teachers, after lengthy consideration, seemed to feel that the effects of divorce were worse than those of the home in which parents were always quarrelling, but all parties were very cautious on the matter owing to lack of precise evidence. The NSPCC, while stating that 'the best place for a child is in its own home', agreed that there comes a time when it is in the child's best interests to remove him. Alternatively, the National Association for Mental Health and the Association of Probation Officers, while admitting lack of clear evidence on this point, both stated that an outright break was better for the child than continual friction. Many witnesses devoted their attention to preservation of marriage rather than its dissolution, suggesting better sex education, marriage guidance and the like.

The Commission deliberated from 1952 till 1956, thus effectively blocking any hopes of legislation for over 4 years. Its report when it eventually came was so hopelessly divided over the major issues that, by convention, substantial reforms were precluded.[25] The radical groups were again the *de facto* losers. The Marriage Law Reform Society declined, and internal disputes further hampered any reformist drive.

The power of Church opinion lasted, and was seen again as late as 1963, when Leo Abse (MP for Pontypool) attempted to introduce a 'divorce after 7 years clause'. Primed by his experiences as a solicitor in Cardiff, he instigated in 1962 a Bill to bring about minor changes in the divorce law. A small band of MPs who saw a need for more radical reforms successfully urged Abse to include a divorce after 7 years' separation clause. Women's organisations rallied to the defence of deserted 'innocent wives', in particular the Church of England's women's group, the Mothers Union, which, fearing that the religious scruples of deserted wives were about to be swept aside, expressed their opposition to the measure in a circular sent to MPs. Their views were taken up by a number of the latter, and the storm aroused caused the sponsors to introduce conciliatory modifications into the Bill.[26] As we have seen, it is not too difficult to block a private member's Bill. Abse, aware that the Conservative majority in the House would probably support the church groups, decided to with-

draw the 7 years clause.[27] Thus conservative pressure groups
allied with Conservative forces within Parliament, were successful in preserving the status quo.

Capital Punishment: a Partial Success

On the whole the 1940s, 1950s and early 1960s were lean
years for the radical reformers. Yet in the realm of penal
reform progress of sorts was made.[28] The Homicide Act of
1957 abolished the death penalty for certain categories of
murderer. The Bill introduced by the Conservative government under Harold Macmillan was a halfway measure which
did not satisfy the true abolitionists, yet something was
achieved and the story behind the Bill is fascinating. To find
its source we have to go back as far as 1923 when the execution of a woman, the first for 17 years, prompted the handful
of penal-reform groups, in particular the highly respected
Howard League for Penal Reform, to form the National Council for the Abolition of the Death Penalty. With a dedicated
secretary, Roy Calvert, and partly financed by the Quaker
chocolate-making firm of Cadbury's, the group got off to a
vigorous start with over eighty meetings held under various
auspices and the production and distribution of eighteen different pamphlets in its first year. Two MPs, Rennie Smith and
Creech Jones, sat on the executive committee, and even at this
stage there was a conspicuous and effective body of intra-parliamentary supporters who during the early months of 1925
embarrassed Home Secretaries with questions the Home Office
was often unable to answer about the comparative murder
statistics from abolitionist countries.[29]

One of the most deeply held popular beliefs was and is
that the death penalty is a deterrent to the potential killer,
but the abolitionists contended that statistics from countries
which had abolished the penalty demonstrated there was no

rise in the murder rate. If the penalty had no deterrent effect, then to the abolitionists it had no justifiable function and was an irrevocable and despairing atrocity. There were difficulties in comparing British and foreign statistics, but in conjunction with continuing pressure on Parliament, Roy Calvert set about compiling a volume to make these comparisons and undermine the deterrent argument. This was published in 1927, and proved its point at least in left-wing circles.[30]

For a year and a half the campaign continued. Outside Parliament there was the distribution of literature, meetings and a petition circulated to ministers of religion and 10,000 local secretaries of political, social and religious organisations— all on an income of just over £1,000pa. Inside Parliament the important struggle for publicity and support continued, with the indefatigable Commander Kenworthy asking questions and attempting to introduce abolitionist measures.[31] The first breakthrough came in December 1928, when his Bill, introduced under the Ten Minute Rule, secured a reading by 119 to 118 votes.[32] There was no time for this Bill to proceed, but support, especially on the Labour benches, was heartening.

The general election of 1929 brought to power the second Labour administration of Ramsay MacDonald. Now the abolitionists were hopeful, and the abolitionist group in the Commons did its best to encourage MPs to enter the ballot and adopt an abolition measure. They were lucky. W. J. Brown won a good place, and there seemed every prospect that the measure would be passed. But the Labour leadership was less enthusiastic than the backbenchers, and the Home Secretary persuaded the Bill's sponsors that it would be wiser to put the matter to a select committee—proceedings with an obvious echo in the 1952 divorce Bill.[33] This committee deliberated for over a year, producing its report in December 1930.[34] Roy Calvert of the National Council was foremost among witnesses, who came from Britain and abroad. The bulk of the British witnesses supported the retention of the death penalty, but the Labour majority on the committee were more convinced by the evidence of Calvert and the abolitionists, and reported in favour of abolition. However, the Conservative group, angered by the handling of the proceedings and less convinced of the desirability of abolition, withdrew from the committee and the ensuing rumpus cast doubt on the credibility of the report.

In the following months abolitionist MPs pressed the government for a debate. The National Council requested an audience with the Home Secretary and was refused. Not surprisingly! Europe by now was suffering from the great depression, and the Labour government was unable to cope. The issue of the death penalty seemed unimportant and unattractive in the face of greater tragedies. In August 1931 the government resigned, Ramsey MacDonald formed a coalition with the Conservatives and the general election reduced the number of Labour seats from 287 to 52. Hope of reform was now gone, and the premature death of Roy Calvert further crippled the campaign. The programme of meetings, pamphlets, parliamentary questions and trial bills continued in muted fashion, until the 1935 election restored Labour fortunes to a more respectable 158 seats. Abolitionist support among MPs was now reckoned at 200, but the Conservative government seemed unlikely to give time for reform and there was no luck to be had in the private members' ballot. Then came World War II.

The post-war story almost convinces one that history repeats itself. In 1945 Labour came to power with a huge majority. The abolitionist MPs, now led by Sidney Silverman, Christopher Hollis and former NCACP secretary, John Paton, was as strong and committed as ever. During 1946 the National Council rebuilt its organisation, its reconstituted executive including Gerald Gardiner, John Paton and Robert Pollard, and new pamphlets were written. But the major impetus again lay within Parliament. The government was confidently expected to introduce a Criminal Justice Bill including reforms on many aspects of penal policy, and the penal-reform group in the Commons decided that the Home Secretary should be pressed to include an abolitionist clause. The Howard League and the National Council collaborated with the parliamentary group, the NC passing the word to other sympathisers to send resolutions to the Home Secretary, arranging a deputation to the Ministry and assisting in sending a circular to MPs. But the Home Secretary, according to the feeling of the deputation which saw him on 7 July 1947, had no strong opinions on the issue, referring the deputation to the 69 per cent of public opinion that apparently opposed abolition, and seeming to be preoccupied by other aspects of his Bill. It appeared unlikely that the Bill itself would contain an abolition clause, but it was understood that there would be no objection to the abolitionists attempting to insert an amendment to that effect. This is what in fact happened. Correspondence from the early weeks of November shows the Council's executive to be in close negotiation with the penal-reform group over the wording of the amendment. It was agreed that it would be politic to opt for suspension for 4 years rather than outright abolition. The Council circularised MPs with abolitionist propaganda.

The amendment was introduced,[35] but the government did not support it. The Home Secretary, Chuter Ede, referred to the weight of public hostility and to his anxiety over the post-war increase in violence, and said that retention was a necessary protection for the police. Several speakers supported this line of argument, but at the vote the abolitionist amendment was carried. The Bill proceeded to the Lords, who rejected the clause with the justification that it was socially dangerous and the public clearly did not want it.[36] For years the duel between the hereditary Lords and the elected Commons had raised the issue of democracy versus privilege. For the Conservative Lords to reject the Bill of a Labour-dominated Commons would have been an open declaration of class war, if the Labour leadership had not always been dubious about the amendment. Its position was thus embarrassing, especially as the hereditary house seemed closer to the will of the people than their elected representatives. The government hastily produced a compromise clause that attempted to grade crimes, with only the most heinous remaining liable to the death penalty. This was also rejected by the Lords as being technically unworkable—a judgment shared by many legal minds.[37] The government's embarrassment was thus increased. It could challenge the Lords on the constitutional point, reintroduce the Bill and use the Parliament Act to force it through. But was this procedure sensible on the eve of a general election and on an issue marginal to Labour policy and unwanted by the electorate? The Prime Minister, Mr Attlee, thought not. He fell back on a Royal Commission. The NCACP admitted tactical defeat, then merged back into the Howard League from which it had sprung.

From the evidence supplied to the Royal Commission (the Gowers Commission) it emerges that the Metropolitan Commissioner of Police and the various police groups—the Chief Constables Association, the Police Federation, the Superintendents Central Committee and the Prison Officers Association—were at that time strongly in favour of retention of the death penalty, if not for all murders at least for armed robbery and any cases in which the deterrent effect might protect the police.[38] Two ex-Home Secretaries supported retention and the Home Office and Law Lords were dubious as to the workability of halfway measures. The Howard League, the Society of Labour Lawyers (represented by Pollard and Gardiner) and the Institute for Psycho-Analysis were the only groups to support abolition. The terms of reference of the

Royal Commission precluded it from direct confrontation with the issue of abolition. Mr Attlee apparently felt this would simply produce a stalemate. The commissioners were to consider whether it was possible to reduce the number of crimes liable to the ultimate penalty, a brief that made their work difficult. The memoranda submitted seem somehow to be deliberating a contrived issue and the report, published in 1953,[39] has the same air. The commissioners, apart from a few minor instances, did not see any ways in which further restriction of the penalty was possible. They accepted the views of the Home Office and judiciary that the idea of degrees of murder would be unworkable. They concluded that the real issue was one of abolition or retention.

Not till February 1955 did the Commons debate the report.[40] The Home Secretary, Major Lloyd George, an abolitionist in 1948, while accepting certain minor reforms, was critical of the commissioners' suggestion that the jury be given more power to determine the sentence. He argued for a mere polite 'taking note' of the report. The abolitionists, however, pressed an amendment to suspend the death penalty for a trial period and were only narrowly defeated.

Later in 1955 the execution of Ruth Ellis for the murder of her lover evoked a fresh wave of humanitarian outrage. In May the general election had again returned the Conservatives, but this was a new generation of them. Churchill had yielded to Eden as Prime Minister and, more significantly, many new Tory members were less instinctively hostile to abolition. The time was ripe for a new initiative. In the summer of 1955, the writer and philosopher Arthur Koestler, together with the left-wing publisher Victor Gollancz, approached the officers of the Howard League to discuss the feasibility of a joint campaign for abolition, and in August the National Campaign for the Abolition of Capital Punishment held its first executive meeting. Those present included

Gollancz, Koestler, Hugh Klare of the Howard League, Gerald Gardiner, Canon Collins and two MPs—Reginald Paget and Christopher Hollis.

Suggestions for action poured out. Campaigns in the press, on television, via the churches and sympathetic bodies such as the Howard League, through the Quakers, local Labour Parties and cooperatives, and a memorial to the Home Secretary, all were suggested; and leaflets, meetings and books were planned, as well as more dramatic methods of protest such as the wearing of mourning on days of execution. The new executive agreed general plans and then delegated their execution to subcommittees of one or two members, with the result that action was taken on most of these fronts over the next weeks. Response to feelers suggested that TV might be interested in suitable scripts and that news coverage of rallies and other actions might be forthcoming. The religious press might be encouraged to take the matter up, and possibly St Paul's Cathedral or Westminster Abbey would hold services on the eve of executions. It was agreed that a public meeting should be held in London in early November 1955, to be followed by other meetings in major provincial cities and by a major effort at the Festival Hall, London, the following spring. Some of these schemes came to naught but the early enthusiasm and drive remain impressive. Nearly 5,000 letters of support arrived at the campaign office (premises provided by Mr Gollancz) within 6 weeks, and over £1,000 was donated. Plans were made to follow up the provincial meetings with the establishment of semi-autonomous local branches.

At this early stage the National Campaign's activities were only loosely integrated with the activities of the penal-reform group in Parliament. There was a prolonged exchange of letters with Lord Chorley over the question of introducing a debate in the Lords.[41] As to the Commons, a string of questions was organised, but in October 1955 a letter from Gardiner to one of the penal-reform group says: 'The question of parliamentary action needs to be tied in.' Later in the month the National Campaign helped the penal-reform group by sending out the customary circular to MPs asking for support in the private members' ballot. By a lucky stroke first place was won by a supporter, but he was too busy to turn up on the appointed day, and his Bill was simply lost—an unusual and tragic event for anyone trying to use the private members' procedure! Sidney Silverman, still unofficial leader of the abolitionist MPs, quickly introduced a Bill under the Ten Minute Rule, but at the time that seemed like an idle gesture.

The countrywide operation of the National Campaign, however, mounted in intensity throughout the winter of 1955-6. In mid-December meetings were being organised in Bristol, Plymouth, Cardiff, Swansea, Leeds and Sheffield. The organisation was efficient, and its support a stupendous 15,000 people, so many that they strained the NC's finances.

The Home Office was not merely passive at this juncture. In 1955 Major Lloyd George had declared himself ready to consider certain limited reforms, and since then consideration had been given to the possibility of introducing a measure which would limit those cases liable to the extreme penalty. Such a scheme had, of course, been considered unworkable by the Gowers Commission, but the government apparently thought otherwise and decided in February 1956 to test the feeling of the House with a motion. The abolitionists naturally considered the proposal half-hearted and began to mobolise support for a policy of outright abolition. The National Campaign executive made arrangements for all MPs to receive campaign literature before the debate, and campaign supporters were urged to write to their MPs. A group in Birmingham sent a petition to the Home Secretary.

The debate was opened by Major Lloyd George, who moved that while the death penalty should remain, the law relating to murder should be amended.[42] A free vote would be allowed on the issue but he urged members in making up their minds to consider two factors: (1) the weight of hostile public opinion, and (2) the responsibility of the legislators to ensure order in the realm. It seems clear that the Home Office was still swayed by the desire of the police to keep the death penalty as a deterrent to the professional gangster. The abolitionists secured the triumph of having Mr Chuter Ede, former Home Secretary, move an amendment calling for experimental abolition. Speakers on both sides rehearsed familiar themes but this time the day was with the abolitionists, their amendment being agreed by 292 votes to 246.

The government had pledged itself to take appropriate action on the outcome of the Commons debate, and optimists thought them now bound to bring in an abolition Bill. Victor Gollancz, listening to the debate from the public gallery, was one of them, and took an instant decision to cancel the whole massive campaign programme; but a week later the government announced that it would not itself introduce an abolition Bill but would make time available for the Bill introduced in November by Sidney Silverman. This action infuriated the reformers. To pilot a private members' Bill past a House of Commons dominated by a hostile administration was no sort of prospect. Supporters urged Mr Silverman to put paid to this plan by withdrawing his Bill, but, being an individualist and a fighter by nature, he decided to take the government at its word.

Outside Parliament the campaign executive met 2 days after the Commons announcement. It felt that there should be some sort of supporting campaign for Mr Silverman's Bill, but its shortage of money meant that priorities had to be weighed very carefully. Considerable discussion ensued over

D

the relative merits of conducting a countrywide campaign or concentrating on parliamentary activity in London. The branches' views were not apparently brought into the discussion. The executive plumped for parliamentary activity, and all meetings except the major one planned for the Festival Hall were cancelled.

The date for the second reading of Mr Silverman's Bill was now fixed for 12 March 1956. The parliamentary group, two of whose members were on the campaign executive, was engaged in consolidating support among the fifty or so Conservative MPs whose continued allegiance was vital to the success of the enterprise. The Campaign executive does not seem to have been formally involved in these activities, but a letter from Christopher Hollis to Gerald Gardiner 10 days before the second reading of the Silverman Bill advised the group not to send more literature to MPs, as it might produce a backlash. The amendment for abolition had only been secured by a combination of a strong Labour vote and the vote of the aforementioned Conservative MPs, who had gone against the official party line. Keeping this group intact was a matter of extreme delicacy.

A certain amount of assistance was given by the National Campaign and by the Howard League in sending out postcards to MPs urging them to attend the crucial divisions on Mr Silverman's Bill, in producing an expert comment on the amendments introduced by the opponents of reform and in distributing abolitionist evidence and propaganda to all MPs during the progress of the Bill. Gerald Gardiner started trying to muster the unpredictable forces of the House of Lords. By writing to likely peers and offering advice, and by securing introductions to peers through Lord Chorley and others with whom contact had already been made, he and the Campaign became a valuable source of expert advice to the abolitionist peers on the statistics of the issue. When Mr

Silverman's Bill passed to the Upper House the Campaign sent much literature and many letters urging the attendance of prospective supporters. A documentary film show was organised for their lordships' benefit and efforts were made to talk to leaders from all quarters of the House. But it was not enough. The Lords, repeating their stand of 1948, rejected the Bill.[43]

Like Mr Attlee's government, the government of 1956 was now in the highly embarrassing position of having to defend a Bill it had never wanted. After consideration it resorted to its original idea of introducing a Bill which would limit the application of the death penalty through the introduction of degrees of murder. This move had several tactical advantages. It was in the Home Office mind a sounder Bill, since it would serve to protect the police against the dangers of armed criminals, it would meet the wishes of at least some of the Tory radicals for a change in the law and by virtue of being different in form from the Silverman Bill it would avert the real constitutional crisis which would have arisen if the Lords rejected the Silverman Bill a second time.

The government leaders then took action along two lines: (1) the preparation during the summer of 1956 of their own Bill, and (2) persuading the radical group of Tory MPs to accept it. In this they were aided by the reactions of constituency parties, which disapproved of abolition and pressed the rebel MPs to toe the constituency line. Many retentionist resolutions were sent forward from constituencies to the Conservative Party Conference. The initiative had passed away from the National Campaign. In the face of public opposition to the reform a popular campaign seemed unlikely to make much headway, and it was decided to attempt to demonstrate through a distinguished persons' memorial that at least 'enlightened' opinion was on the side of reform. Even this did not alter the government's decision. Its Bill was introduced.

The National Campaign executive responded by publishing a leaflet outlining the difficulties and apparent illogicalities of trying to distinguish between degrees of murder, and sent it to all Conservative abolitionists and to Labour supporters who might speak in the forthcoming debates. But now no one entertained any hope that it would be possible to convert the Bill into a thoroughgoing abolitionist measure. The Homicide Bill, as it was called, passed into law without amendment and the National Campaign never recovered its former glory.

The Lessons Learned

This chapter may be the despair of the fringe-group campaigner, for it demonstrates just how difficult it can be for the small pressure groups to penetrate Westminster and to succeed via the private member's Bill. Groups can do little while Parliament is hostile. For instance, the Labour backbenchers were sympathetic to abolition even in the 1930s, but their support for this and for other 'moral' reforms was crowded out by the pressing urgency of the country's economic situation both in 1930 and in 1945-51, and by the party leadership's lack of enthusiasm for reform. Where pressure built up, and where there seemed to be a possibility that the reformers would be successful (capital punishment in 1929 and 1948 and divorce law reform in 1951), the government's decision to establish committee or commission effectively inhibited further developments. The committee findings were hostile to abortion reform, and on capital punishment in 1929 and divorce in 1956 the reports were divided and ineffective. An anti-reformist report is a good reason for government apathy, but even where the report is sympathetic, as were the Wolfenden Committee's proposals on homosexuality in 1957, the government need not take action if it does not choose. In fact for nearly 10 years reformers trying to build on Wolfenden met precisely the same blocking tactics as did those of the other groups. Government hostility to reform was in the main sufficient to curtail the efforts of sympathetic MPs to that of the occasional question or deputation.

Without support from MPs and peers groups have no hope of generating legislation. Yet even sympathetic MPs are not the delegates of groups, and the difficulties ALRA experienced with Lord Amulree in 1953 are echoed by the differences between the divorce and homosexual law reformers and their champion Leo Abse. However, even if an MP is willing to sponsor a Bill there is relatively little hope of its being successful, given the miniscule allotment of time to private members and the relative ease with which opponents can prevent the debate from reaching a vote.

This chapter has highlighted the difficulties besetting outgroups, but their relative lack of success does not necessarily mean that pressure groups on moral issues were totally ineffective in this period. The failure of the reforms is in a sense the success of the conservatives—of the opinions of church, the medical profession and the police. Police groups were perhaps the most active in their sustained pressure on the Home Office to retain the death penalty for certain categories for murder. Their representations weighed heavily with all governments of the period. The other established groups were, however, far less active, simply presenting their highly acceptable views to the committees and commissions. The radical groups were no significant threat to them and they did not find it necessary to wage persistent and active campaigns. Their effectiveness derived in the main from the fact that their values were tacitly embodied in the norms and assumptions of everyday life.

The case of capital punishment shows that the Conservative government was not implacably hostile to reform, yet it reinforces the overriding importance of government and Parliament. Until 1955 the reformers suffered the same setbacks as other groups. Thereafter opinion began to move in their direction, but the significant factors are those inside Parliament—the Labour Party's dedication to abolition, and the Conservative government's move towards reform. How much did the extra-parliamentary pressure groups contribute to this process? The 1955 campaign provided a valuable service, particularly in providing literature and evidence to radical peers for the debates, but one cannot forget the long-standing existence of the penal-reform group in the Commons, whose dedication was essential for the passage of Mr Silverman's Bill. Contact between this group and the extra-parliamentary campaign was fairly close, but the campaigners were the junior partners. Probably the most important contributions made by the pressure groups came in their apparently least successful phase back in the late 1920s, with the initial assembling of the anti-deterrent argument by Roy Calvert, and the efforts of the group to convert Labour Party opinion.

Notes to this chapter are on p169

3 The Organisation of the Rival Groups

In Chapter 2 we encountered some of the groups that made a stand over moral issues of the 1950s and 1960s. In all they must have numbered well over 100. What sort of groups were they, how did they operate and were they 'democratic'? Roughly the opposition to reform came from institutionalised groups such as the Church of England and the Police Federation, while support for reform came from small non-establishment groups like the Abortion Law Reform Association or National Secular Society.

Institutionalised Groups

The most obvious and consistent opponents of the abolition of capital punishment were the professional associations of police and prison officers—the Chief Constables Association, the Superintendents Central Committee, the Police Federation and the Prison Officers Association. All these supported retention for some if not all capital crimes in their memoranda to the Royal Commission of 1949, and the last two held this position to the end in 1965. Church groups did not make much of a stand against retention in 1949, though the Association of Prison Chaplains stated: 'Society . . . may act

55

on behalf of God. In the matter of evil doers it has a God given right to check and correct any subversive elements . . . and in extreme cases . . . to remove the offenders by death.'

On the question of divorce it was the Church of England, especially its Mothers Union, which provided the most effective brake on reform. At the time of the 1952 Royal Commission on Marriage and Divorce it was supported by the Bar Council, by church groups from other denominations and in some measure by certain educational groups. In later years, when the Bills were struggling through Parliament, the Mothers Union, the Baptist Union and the Married Women's Association provided the fiercest opposition. The Roman Catholic Church did not offer strong opposition to marriage or divorce reforms but was, among church groups, one of the most determined opponents of reform of the law on abortion, working through a variety of subsections of the Catholic church, such as the Lamp Society, the Catholic Women's League, the Union of Catholic Mothers, the Guild of Saint Luke and Saint Dunstan, and the Catholic Doctors' Guild. Also on this particular issue extremely important and effective opposition came from the leading professional associations of medical men—the British Medical Association and the Royal College of Obstetricians and Gynaecologists.

Though not totally opposed to reform, it was these church, medical and police groups that most consistently made out the counter case and counselled moderation. They were all well established organisations with a legitimate brief to speak authoritatively on matters which so obviously fell within their province. They were all multi-purpose organisations, not just concerned with these single-issue campaigns. Each had an extensive organisation aimed at incorporating major sections of the population. The Mothers Union alone claimed nearly 400,000 members in 1968 and the Police Federation in 1964 had 80,040. The medical groups were generally smaller but, more importantly, were the recognised leaders of their profession, representing more than 80 per cent of medical men and women.

Like most organisations these institutionalised groups were mainly led from the top, though they had constitutional channels for policy endorsement and suggestions from the lower ranks. The police groups in preparing their submissions for the 1949 Royal Commission systematically collected the opinions of their constituent branches. The church and medical groups, however, tended to set up high-level working parties to produce policy statements which rank and file could only endorse or reject at annual general meetings. When it came to negotiations with governments or the sponsors of Bills, group leaders acted independently without systematic reference back to the general membership. The oligarchic tendency does not, of course, automatically prevent representatives from reflecting the views of their members. The policy documents were generally approved by the annual general assemblies. The majority vote at the BMA annual conference in July 1967 in favour of the Abortion Bill's terms was presumably an endorsement of BMA executive efforts; and a survey of the views of members of the Royal College of Obstetricians and Gynaecologists taken a year after the Act suggests that members largely agreed with RCOG policy.[1] It is more difficult to know how far the views of the high echelons of the Church of England and other denominational groups actually equated with those of the laity, but it is fair to say that these institutionalised groups were, within culturally acceptable limits, representative of their members.

In addition they had all achieved the accolade of respectability. Headed by upper-class and staffed by middle-class professionals, they were respectable bodies which had been involved in negotiations with government departments on many issues over a number of years. The medical and police professions stood in a special relation to government by virtue of being state employees. All these groups accepted the political system and the practice of reform by constitutional means. In the end their years of relative security and lack of aggressive campaigning may have been a disadvantage to them when faced by the fervour of the radical groups allied to the support of the Labour government.

Radical Groups

At first sight, however, the radical groups opposed to these forces seem puny. All of them followed the stereotype of pressure groups as a middle-class phenomenon founded by one or two professional people with some prior experience of campaigning on unpopular issues (German refugees, birth control, votes for women, church disestablishment) who had decided that the time had come to launch yet another campaign. There is no indication that they chose particularly auspicious times; it depended more on personal zeal in conjunction with available time and money. Each founder recruited half a dozen or so persons of similar social background and experience; and from then on, however much these movements grew, and though some disciples fell away, it was basically the founder and his early recruits who ran the organisation, carried out its programme and achieved whatever the group finally did achieve. The 'middle-classness' and professional training of the central figures profoundly affected the type of pressure group that emerged. For their time they were radical and daring people: several were the children of clergymen, heirs to the radical humanitarian thread in British social life; others, such as Robert Pollard, founder of the MLRS, or Victor Gollancz of the National Campaign, were more than a little acquainted with left-wing political ideas. However, the cast of these groups was typically British, typically Fabian, typically reformist. This affected their choice of aims. As treasurer and historian of the Marriage Law Reform Society, Stephen Keleney wrote: 'At first there were two conflicting schools of thought: some wished to conduct general propaganda for fundamental reforms of the institution of marriage . . . while others were of the opinion that we must concentrate on such aims which have some chance of being enacted . . . at least within the lifetime of the members present. The latter school of thought prevailed.'[2] Each group, then, adopted a fairly narrow focus of interest, accepting that it was possible to effect certain small changes in the world without disrupting the social structure.

This reformist approach also dominated the groups' choice of tactics. A group that wants freer abortion, fewer executions or just to build a bridge or keep a school open, has a large range of possible courses of action. The primary choice is between direct and indirect action. Many welfare and amenity groups combine direct action—eg, help for the disabled—with political pressure for a better deal for all the disadvantaged. Direct action has become increasingly prevalent in recent years, culminating in the 1970s in the no-go areas in various cities in Northern Ireland. However, the pressure groups of the 1950s eschewed direct action—performing abortions, mercy-killing, etc—not just because of the practical difficulties but also because they did not wish to break the law. Like most of us they respected the law in general, even where they disagreed with it in detail. They saw their task not as one of directly changing behaviour but as one of changing the law which circumscribed behaviour.

However, though law reform by legal means was their objective, they all became involved in social service work willynilly; for as soon as they publicised their particular programmes, they started getting letters from such people as women wanting abortions, desperate homosexuals, men unable to obtain divorces from dependent wives, and families of condemned prisoners. Some chronic sick even wrote to the Voluntary Euthanasia Society, hoping to relieve their suffering. Only the Homosexual Law Reform Society institutionalised its commitment to social work, setting up in parallel with another law-reform society, the Albany Trust, which eventually acquired its own social worker. In other groups the executive could only cope with the desperate pleas they received by burning the midnight oil over replies offering such advice as was consistent with the existing law. Inevitably the issues were tricky at times.

Groups oriented to law reform can work either through parliament or, as was often done over civil rights in the United States, through the courts. However, the courts are more useful when one aims at restitution of rights that are being abrogated than where one is trying to change the rights themselves. Only the Abortion Law Reform Association seriously considered trying to change case law, and even they did not actively pursue the policy.

Most of the radical groups, therefore, might be described as single-issue law reform groups. What methods did they use to impress parliament of the need for reform? Of recent years protests have become increasingly dramatic, beginning with the sit-downs and break-ins of the Committee of One Hundred and carrying on through the squatter movement of the late 1960s to citizens hurling stones and using firearms on each other in the streets of Ulster. Admittedly in the 1950s there were always a few executive members prepared to argue for the dramatic gesture designed to catch the eye and irritate the government into action. Thus Arthur Koestler of the capital-punishment campaign suggested wearing black armbands and calling a curfew on the eve of executions, and some sections of the Marriage Law Reform Society wanted to call a maintenance strike and stage demonstrations at weddings. All the groups had the opportunity to capitalise on certain sad cases which inevitably came to their notice. However, the majority on each executive favoured more orthodox and less emotive tactics. The main weapon was that of producing pamphlets aimed at MPs and other opinion leaders and in trying to persuade well disposed MPs to introduce Bills and motions into Parliament. Open meetings with distinguished speakers were also favoured for spreading the word, and petitions and letters to all MPs were mobilised at certain stages of the campaign. Apart from a parade of sandwich-board men in 1951 in support of divorce law reform, there were no mass marches of the sort so monotonously common today.

So, these groups started out virtually as groups of friends who believed that 'something should be done'. In their early meetings, generally held monthly, they were hectically busy approving pamphlets stating their aims, building a panel of distinguished supporters for their letterheads, and arranging inaugural meetings. All of them had some degree of formality in the keeping of minutes and the allocating of posts, but the atmosphere was predominantly informal and exciting. Keleney of the Marriage Law Reform Committee organisation wrote:

> Our committee meetings were most friendly, informal and efficient, or at least effective gatherings. Without any very fixed rules of procedure, we managed to make all the decisions almost unanimously and shared out the work among members of the Committee. The greatest merit in keeping the organisation group belongs . . . to the Chairman, Robert Pollard, who seems to have an extraordinary talent for driving a most heterogeneous team, smoothly and consistently.[3]

One interesting fact is that, with the possible exception of the capital-punishment reformers, none of the groups imagined themselves acquiring a mass membership. The largest was the National Campaign for the Abolition of Capital Punishment, which at its height in 1955-6 counted 30,000 supporters, but this organisational phase was extremely short-lived and in subsequent years regular paying supporters numbered only a few hundred. The executive of the Homosexual Law Reform Society, worried lest the organisation should become dominated by homosexuals who might ruin the society's image and chances of success, deliberately left the status of their supporters vague. They continually sought subscribers, especially among the wealthy, but had no category of official membership. Support can be roughly estimated at around 2,000 at peak. All the organisations increased in membership when they seemed likely to be successful. The MLRS grew to around 1,500 in 1951-2, when it was engaged on a big parliamentary offensive. Initially its members came largely from radicals in the Progressive League who learned of its existence from personal contacts, but later it gathered recruits from unexpected sources, as when Marcus Lipton, an MP fighting for divorce reform in the Commons, received hundreds of letters from sufferers under the existing law, many of whom later became members of MLRS. The founder of the Voluntary Euthanasia Society was a great believer in the weight of 'upper-class' opinion, and by systematically writing to people in *Who's Who* he built up in the early years a list of over 1,000 distinguished supporters. But this policy was discontinued after his death and membership fell to the low hundreds. VES had 500 in the late 1960s. ALRA's membership fell similarly, then rose to around 2,000. These reformist organisations all lacked the countrywide network of local branches and support that characterised the church and professional groups. Admittedly they sprouted a handful of branches at times when success seemed possible but these were not integrated into any bureaucratic network and bear no comparison to the stable organisation of the counter groups.

Apart from the National Campaign for the Abolition of

Capital Punishment and the Homosexual Law Reform Society, the other groups held AGMs and to some extent tried to take members' views into account. A few individual members performed independent and sterling work for their groups in lecturing or fund-raising, but generally members were willing to delegate all their responsibilities to the central committee.

The counter groups were staffed by full-time administrations of some size and importance. The reformist groups were not. The National Campaign and the HLRS had full-time administrators and several secretarial staff, though in the former case for only a few months; the other groups also in time acquired some paid secretarial assistance but none of this eroded their central structure, which was the power of the executive committee of volunteers. These committees, which re-elected themselves every year and saw to the replacement of such of their number as died or gave up through pressure of other activities, carried the brunt of group decision-making and activity and sank not inconsiderable amounts of time and money into their cause.

The small membership of radical pressure groups, in this elitist world, was counterbalanced by the quality and social connections of their leaders. The National Campaign committee was stacked with notables, as we have seen, with Victor Gollancz as chairman and Arthur Koestler and Gerald Gardiner, QC (a later Lord Chancellor) on its executive. Other groups were perhaps less spectacular in their casting, but the Homosexual Law Reform Society executive included Kenneth Robinson (later Minister of Health in the 1964 Labour government), Jeremy Thorpe, Leader of the Liberal Party, and Leo Abse, MP, whose Bill eventually became law. ALRA was always led by experienced campaigners, and improved its contacts over the years, being especially fortunate to have as chairman Mrs Vera Houghton, a well known campaigner for the International Federation for Planned Parenthood and also wife of the minister with general responsibility for social services in the 1964 Labour government. The divorce and euthanasia campaigners were perhaps less well connected, but were still led by persons of some skill and social standing.

While it is useful to generalise that the institutional groups were large and legitimate, while the reforming groups were small and illegitimate, some exceptions should be noticed. Over the years, as the former became more liberal in their opinions or apparently less effective in defending established positions, one or two small conservative groups like the Society for the Protection of the Unborn Child or the Anti-Violence League, a retentionist group, sprang up. These were constituted and run like the radical groups. They lacked money and legitimacy, and were generally not very successful. Conversely, some radical groups, were established and bureaucratic. Most notable was the Howard League for Penal Reform, a respected if small group with a tradition of giving sensible reformist advice on penal matters. This group did much discreet work for the abolitionist cause, producing pamphlets and talking to MPs and peers. Also there were women's groups like the Women's Co-operative Guild and the Family Planning Association, large federations whose executives purported to speak for several thousand women. However, their support for the radical cause was mainly confined to passing resolutions. The National Council of Women also intermittently supported reforms but, having several church organisations such as the MU as constituent members, its views tended to fluctuate according to the strength of the factions within it.

Notes to this chapter are on p171

4 *In Which Pressure Groups Appear to Be Successful*

The making of a law requires a text, a sponsor, a debate, a committee, another debate, a constant spate of amendments, a flurry of Whips and perhaps an all-night sitting, before victory is won. It is a gruelling, frustrating procedure. What role do pressure groups play in it? The circumstances surrounding a private member's Bill are, as we have noted earlier, different from those of government Bills, and, just to add to the variety, members' bills differ widely from each other. Some Bills seem to attract a large amount of pressure-group activity. Others pass into law with virtually none. The Murder Bill of 1965 was an example of the latter category, the Divorce Bill of 1969 an example of moderate activity and the Medical Termination of Pregnancy Bill the focus of considerable activity. More important, however, than the sheer volume of group activity generated by a Bill is the fact that there are all sorts of different ways of participating, some of them more strenuous than others. They range from direct determination of the Bill's central contents to the mere polite letter of enquiry about a Bill's effects. These differences will emerge in the following case studies.

E

The Murder Bill

As we have said, the Murder Bill, which provisionally abolished the death penalty, passed into law with relatively little pressure-group activity. We saw in Chapter 2 how abolitionist efforts were foiled over a period of 40 years by a combination of circumstances, in particular the opposition of police and public. After the Homicide Act of 1957 the National Campaign for the Abolition of Capital Punishment cut back its activities, and for 2–3 years was little more than an address in the telephone directory. In the early 1960s there seemed a chance that the Homicide Act might be rescinded, and the campaign then became somewhat more active, but its efforts were counter-balanced by a shortlived and oddly named retentionist group, the Anti-Violence League. The Prime Minister did not favour any change and this, together with adverse public opinion and Tory backbench hostility precluded any alterations to the statute. The National Campaign relapsed into virtual inactivity once more, holding only the occasional committee meeting.

In 1963 the fortunes of the Conservative party reached a low ebb. A Labour victory seemed increasingly likely in the next general election, and the massive support in that party for abolition meant that it was almost a certainty, provided facilities were available for a Bill. In fact, in a meeting just before the election the National Campaign committee, which now included Sidney Silverman himself, discussed the mechanics of the private members' Bill procedure. After the election the new Labour government's small majority caused the committee to fear for the prospects of an abolition Bill. However Gerald Gardiner, long-standing member of the abolitionist groups, agreed to accept the office of Lord Chancellor in the new administration. As is customary he resigned his external committee posts, including that of vice-chairman of the National Campaign, but this official gesture in no way detracted from his devotion to the cause. Thereafter the National Campaign for the Abolition of Capital Punishment appears to have done little or nothing.

Lord Gardiner probably had little difficulty in persuading his colleagues of the desirability of introducing an abolition Bill, and in fact it was mentioned in the Queen's Speech. The Bill did not become official government policy, the speech from the throne merely recording that time would be made available during the session for a private member's abolition Bill; but it would not have to undergo the vagaries of the ballot, an exemption which was a decisive advantage.

Lord Gardiner and Mr Silverman already had a draft text in preparation, and after some discussion with government officers it was decided to confine its terms to the most elementary necessities. The Bill was reduced to three principles—abolition, life imprisonment and a date of operation. All three produced difficulties. The Bill secured a second reading by a massive vote from the Labour benches, and as it was one of the first important votes of the session, it had great symbolic significance for the newly elected Labour Party. It proceeded, as Bills normally do, to a subcommittee for the process of clause by clause scrutiny, but by manipulation of a perfectly lawful procedural device was recalled to the floor of the House, which meant that the committee stage had to begin all over again. A Bill in the British Parliament has to pass through a series of stages in both the House of Commons and the House of Lords within 1 parliamentary year if it is to become law. The timetable is always tight and delays can be fatal. Thus events put the Murder Bill in jeopardy, and to safeguard its passage the cabinet, which controls the parliamentary timetable, took the unusual step of granting extra morning sessions.

Public opinion polls taken at the time demonstrated the public's continuing hostility to abolition.[1] Over 65 per cent felt that the penalty should be retained, but the Anti-Violence

Campaign of the early 1960s was not resurrected to fight the Bill nor did any other similar group make a conspicuous impression. The most noteworthy organised opposition came from the Police Federation and the Prison Officers Association, both of which quietly made representations to the Home Office and to MPs, but efforts in both Houses to retain execution for murders of members of these groups were rejected. The only major Commons amendment determined that the Bill should remain in force for only 5 years. In moving it Henry (later Lord) Brooke was giving heed to the weight of public opinion opposed to abolition.

Prolonged argument occurred over what sentence should replace the death penalty. Abolitionists generally felt it should be life imprisonment, with the Home Secretary having the discretion to remit part of the sentence if he thought fit. Others felt that the trial judge should be empowered to specify the sentence, so that the horror of the crime could be reflected in the severity of its punishment. Many felt that a life sentence (effectively 8 or 9 years) was too light for some of the more horrific murders. The Lord Chief Justice, Lord Parker, had for some years been arguing for stiffer sentences, and when the Bill reached the Lords, succeeded in moving an amendment in committee giving the court discretion over the sentence. At the report stage he replaced this with a solution privately suggested by Gerald Gardiner as long ago as 1962 whereby the sentence would be life imprisonment with the added proviso that the court could at the time of sentencing recommend to the Home Secretary the minimum period of detention. Lord Parker also secured an amendment agreed by the sponsors concerning conditions for parole.

One should not, of course, ignore the role played by abolitionist and retentionist campaigns over the years, but the fact remains that the passage of the Murder Bill secured singularly little attention from such groups despite the fact that 65 per cent of the population opposed the reform in the opinion polls.

Abortion Law Reform

As we have seen, until 1961 ALRA was a voice crying in the wilderness. In the late 1950s, however, social attitudes began to change more rapidly. The defeat at Suez in 1956 and the end of Empire were coupled with the coming of the youth culture, which, having sex as a central if latent element, prompted changes in attitudes and standards of behaviour. On television the satirical programme *TW3* broke through all the old tabus, and the consumer boom which in 1959 enabled the Prime Minister, Harold Macmillan, to secure the return of the Conservatives to office signalled a casting aside of restriction and an indulgence in materialism associated with secular rather than religious values. The new values had as yet not extended to abortion reform, but in 1961 the fortuitous calamity of Thalidomide provided an effective catalyst.

Thalidomide was a tranquillising drug, assumed to be safe but actually prone to produce deformity of the foetus when taken by pregnant women. It was withdrawn from the market but too late for some 400 British mothers-to-be, who faced the prospect of giving birth to a badly handicapped child. Their sad situation kindled the sympathy of public and press and a Gallup poll showed 61 per cent support for a Belgian mother who had killed her deformed infant. Questions asked in the British Parliament by Edith Summerskill, however, elicited the government view that it would be inappropriate to amend the law on abortion. Nor did the Thalidomide affair produce any instant reassessment among the medical or clerical professions, nor, surprisingly, much response from the executive of the Abortion Law Reform Association—a fact sufficient to irritate into militancy a small handful of members who, taking over the reins of the Association, became the spearhead of a purposeful, intelligent and ultimately successful drive for reform.

For the next few years ALRA gathered its strength and intensified its activities.[2] Branches developed spontaneously in various parts of the country, but the central driving force was the voluntary committee in London, which embarked on a vigorous programme of public speaking, advertising and propagandising (especially among women's organisations and in the media). The period 1961–4 saw an unparalleled expansion of publicity, in fact, for the abortion issue in the news, letter and feature columns of magazines and newspapers, much of it ALRA-inspired, though around this time the press itself began to speak with new freedom and frankness on moral matters. The ALRA annual report records a debt to 'feature writers and journalists who have taken up the fight for abortion law reform'. One of ALRA's master strokes was its use of the public opinion poll. A survey of GPs initiated by the North West London branch recorded that 70 per cent of respondents approved of ALRA's aims, but since these results were based on only little more than a 30 per cent response, it is doubtful how much attention should have been paid to them. They were, however, an effective propaganda weapon and led to further, more reliable, surveys.

The newly elected Parliament of 1964 contained, by ALRA's calculations, 150 supporters of reform (significant but hardly enough to carry a Bill). The Home Secretary Frank Soskice, when approached by ALRA, was hesitant about reform. Perhaps mindful of the government's tiny minority, he seemed unsure whether abortion law reform would enjoy public sympathy. In fact, an opinion poll in March 1965 showed majority support for abortion in cases of rape (61 per cent) and deformity (58 per cent).[3] Only minorities at this stage supported abortion to prevent the birth of an illegitimate child (15 per cent) or in cases of financial hardship (36 per cent). Later in the year both the BMA and the Church of England, almost certainly prompted by the gathering momentum of the ALRA campaign, decided without much enthusiasm to set up working parties to consider the question, but in the autumn of 1965, before these groups could reach a conclusion, ALRA seized an important initiative in the shape of Lord Silkin's Bill. This, the first of a series of abortion Bills, was eventually lost when the government, seeking to improve its dangerously small majority, went to the country in March 1966, but its history presents an almost classic case of pressure by various types of group. Moves and counter moves between ALRA, the British Medical Association, the Royal College of Obstetricians and Gynaecologists, the Home Office and the leading spokesmen among the peers took a form which was substantially repeated in a later session during the passage of the ultimately successful Bill introduced by David Steel. We shall therefore consider Lord Silkin's Bill and what happened to it.

As there is no equivalent in the Lords to the ballot system, it is easier for a group to get a Bill introduced there than in the Commons, but very few of them are ever enacted, since there is rarely time for them to proceed from the Lords through the Commons in the same session. Nonetheless such attempts have many important functions. Lord Silkin decided to hazard an abortion Bill after a chance meeting with an ALRA supporter. As is normal with non-government Bills, he as sponsor had to produce a first draft to put before the legislature, and in this case the draft was supplied by ALRA's leading legal adviser, Prof Glanville Williams. Its principal clauses provided for termination of pregnancy by any registered medical practitioner, (1) to avert grave risk to the patient's physical or mental health (ie, a codification of the Bourne judgment), (2) to avert the possible birth of a grossly deformed child, and (3) 'In the belief that the health of the patient or the social conditions in which she is living' made her unsuitable to bear the child (hereafter referred to as the social clause) where the pregnancy resulted from a sexual offence or the patient was of unsound mind. The Bill overcame its first major hurdle of the second reading by a comfortable majority, but not before several peers had expressed disquiet over its details and Lord Silkin had agreed to engage in discussions over them. He acceded even at this early stage to the view that a second opinion was desirable before abortions were performed, even though under existing practice the opinion of a single doctor was sufficient.

The leading critic of the Bill was Lord Dilhorne, Lord Chancellor in the previous government. He acted no doubt on the basis of personal convictions, but these had much in common with leading opinion in the medical profession, and he was shortly reported in the medical press as engaged in discussions with leaders of the BMA. Lord Silkin, too, was approached by the BMA and ALRA leaders kept in constant contact to monitor any reactionary moves.

At the end of December 1965, while these discussions were in progress the Church of England working party produced its report,[4] which submitted that 'in certain circumstances abortion can be justified where it could reasonably be established that there was a threat to the mother's life or well-being and hence inescapably to her health', and added later that, in determining the risk to the mother, account could be taken of the 'patient's total environment, actual or reasonably foreseeable'. Foetal abnormality, rape or social conditions were thus inadmissible grounds unless they were clearly having detrimental effects on the woman. In one sense the Church of England had not moved far from the traditional position (by which threat to the mother's health was the sole justification for violating the foetus). However, it had advanced slightly in talking about the mother's 'well-being' and also of the patient's environment 'actual, or reasonably foreseeable'; and had perhaps unwittingly widened the range of factors that might be considered to constitute a risk. Lord Silkin decided to follow this lead by adding the 'total environment' formula to his 'health of the mother' clause, but, the church notwithstanding, he was still bent on retaining the other provisions as well. Thus the Bill became temporarily even more liberal.

Restrictive pressures were soon in evidence, however, with the publication of a preliminary statement by the BMA committee.[5] Its restrictions concerned both the grounds for the operation and the technical circumstances of by whom and where. All parties agreed throughout the negotiations that abortions should only be performed by trained medical men, but the statements of the medical profession were always such as to emphasise that it was their sole right to sanction where and by whom abortions could be performed and that this should be done on medical grounds alone. At this stage the BMA view was that there should be two doctors consenting to the operation, that it should be performed in an NHS hospital or place specially registered for the purpose and, most restrictive of all, that it should be performed only by or under a consultant gynaecologist. All these requirements were more restrictive than the existing law, under which any GP could legally perform the operation anywhere if the grounds were sufficient. The stipulation about the gynaecologist was particularly restricting in view of the generally traditional attitude of this group and its small number. As to admissible grounds, the BMA explicitly accepted the existing grounds of risk to life and health of the mother and adopted the Church of England formulation concerning circumstances relevant to assessing that risk; in addition it accepted foetal disease and, with some misgivings, sexual offence as new and independent grounds for abortion. Abortion for social reasons was not mentioned, and by implication rejected. Lines were drawn, therefore, between ALRA pressing for liberal reforms and the medical groups seeking to impose numerous safeguards. The subsequent history of reform charts the swaying fortunes of these positions.

Initially Lord Silkin was unwilling to concede more to the BMA than that there should be two consenting opinions, but at the committee stage of his Bill he agreed to tighten this to two doctors, one with an NHS appointment. Later he added two conditions desired by both the BMA and the Ministry of Health, that the operation should take place only in NHS hospitals or places approved by the Ministry, and that the operation should be performed by a practitioner with an appointment in an NHS hospital of at least the status of registrar. Thus the medical groups had apparently made a significant impact on the framing of technical provisions.

Their views also carried some weight on the question of admissible grounds. It was generally argued by medical men and church alike that there were cases such as anencephalic children where abortion would be appropriate. The whole problem was to devise a form of words that would include these but not (paradoxically) cases such as Thalidomide babies, who, despite their handicaps, had a prospect of a reasonable existence. The medical peers seemed anxious for the profession to retain discretion and disliked the introduction of non-medical formulations such as 'enjoyment of life' (suggested by Dilhorne). Ultimately a definition they considered workable was incorporated. As to other causes, the medical groups assumed the right of the profession to decide whether a particular case should be aborted and in consequence insisted that medical reasons alone should be the determining factors. The BMA declared: 'Quite apart from the difficulties of definition we do not think that termination is justifiable on grounds of physical or mental inadequacy to be a mother'. A majority of peers agreed that social inadequacy was not a matter to be taken into consideration, and the social clause was voted out of the Bill. So, too, was the sexual offences clause, probably because of Home Office advice that it would not be workable. Then the whole Bill was lost because of the 1966 general election.

The original Bill, which it is not too misleading to call an ALRA Bill, had been modified, sometimes with ALRA's support, by several pressures. The status of the doctors and hospitals involved had been settled by incorporating suggestions from the medical profession and the Home Office. On the grounds admissible, the medical men had come up with a form of words to cover the clause concerning foetal abnormality; abortion in cases of rape had been rejected by Home Office and medical reasoning; and the clause dealing with social reasons for abortion, about which both doctors and the Church of England were dubious, had been dropped for a formula devised by the latter.

At this point the General Council of the Royal College of Obstetricians and Gynaecologists, long active behind the scenes, issued a tough official statement.[6] The RCOG doubted the need for any abortion Bill at all, but if there was to be one, the grounds allowed should be the mental and physical health of the mother or the prospect of serious handicap in the foetus. No social or rape clause was supported. The final sting was the RCOG's demand that the operation should only be carried out by a consultant obstetrician or gynaecologist under contract to the NHS, or his nominee, in an NHS hospital or place approved after agreement by two NHS consultants, one of whom would perform the operation. This demand, which was actually accepted by the Ministry of Health and by Lord Silkin, who incorporated it in his Bill introduced in the new session of Parliament, was not supported wholeheartedly by the rest of the medical profession. The BMA represented a wider medical opinion than the College, and clearly many of its members saw no need to restrict control of the operation to the highest ranks of the profession; they also began to defend the view that it should be possible for doctors working outside the NHS to perform the operation. The BMA and RCOG set up a joint committee to consider their differences on this point. The RCOG view appears to have dominated, in that the final report recommended a consultant with NHS appointment, though the RCOG still felt that a gynaecological consultant should be stipulated.[7] The two sections of the profession were agreed on the desirability of restricting the grounds for abortion to the health of the mother (though by adding the Church of England formula a liberal interpretation was possible, if unintended) and to cases of serious abnormality. The Royal Medico-Psychological Association on the other hand argued that, in addition to the traditionally accepted medical and psychiatric circumstances, all social circumstances should be taken into account. This liberal representation seems to have counted for little beside those of the better known medical bodies.

The general election of 1966 returned a Labour government with a convincing majority. The Labour Party, with its strong working-class connections, is not automatically the party of liberal reforms in spheres of personal morality, but many of its members, especially Labour intellectuals, strongly defend the individual's freedom in moral matters. The coming of the 1966 Labour administration, therefore, was probably the most significant single factor in facilitating the passage of reformist bills. In 1964 ALRA had counted 150 MPs as supporters, but by February 1966 this had risen to 400. Much of this increase must have been due to efforts of certain members of the ALRA committee who over a long period simply went into the lobby at Westminster to talk to MPs. Support for abortion-law reform was thus growing in the Commons, but everything hung on success in the ballot for private members' time.

On the crucial day ALRA's representatives went to the House and secured the attention of one of the lucky winners,

David Steel, member of the Liberal Party. They urged him to adopt abortion law reform, and, after consulting his constituency and with informal support from the Home Secretary, he agreed to do so. The history of Steel's Bill parallels that of Lord Silkin's. The first draft was the product of a committee on which ALRA had powerful representation, and Simms and Hindell, ALRA's biographers, give an inside account of the drafting.[8] As we have seen, there were two major issues in the Bill—the technical provisions surrounding the operation of abortion, and the grounds on which it could be performed. In Steel's Bill the operation could be performed by any registered medical practitioner, with the assent of another, in an NHS hospital or approved nursing home. This provision failed to meet ALRA's wish that the existing situation, in which no assenting opinion was automatically necessary, might prevail, but was much less restrictive than the RCOG amendments that had found their way into Lord Silkin's Bill. Steel adopted the same four basic grounds for abortion as appeared in that Bill originally—health of mother, eugenic reasons, the social clause and rape. The Home Office disapproved of abortion for rape victims, but ALRA persuaded the sponsor to include it. Thus we are virtually back to square one and the same battles had to be fought all over again.

At the second reading Roman Catholic MPs, supported in the background by Roman Catholic organisations and by some vigorous gynaecologists, opposed the bill on religious, medical and humanitarian grounds, but the reformers carried the day. After the debate there was a long interlude, which made the reformers fear the Bill would be lost through lack of time, but this threat was averted when sympathetic forces in the government transferred it to another committee.

In the interim Steel had had meetings with representatives of the medical groups, and, despite strong counter pressure from ALRA, decided to make changes in the clauses specifying

the grounds for abortion similar to those in Lord Silkin's Bill.
The first provision was thus widened so that abortion became
permissible if the pregnancy involved a risk to the woman's
'well-being' (not just to her physical or mental health); and in
determining that risk a doctor could take into account the
'patient's total environment, actual or reasonably foreseeable'.
This done, Steel decided the separate rape and social clauses
could be dropped, reasoning, according to Simms and Hindell,
that the Bill's chances would be improved if it was known to
be in line with the expressed opinions of the church and medical bodies, which had stressed continuously that the granting
of abortion should depend on medical, not social, circumstances.[9] Steel introduced these changes at the committee stage,
and another committee member, Edward Lyons, added that
besides considering risk to the mother's health and well-being
the doctor could consider whether the continued pregnancy
involved risk to the 'future well-being of the child or her other
children'. The medical groups, dominated by the Royal College
of Obstetricians and Gynaecologists, and supported by the
Ministry of Health, took exception to Steel's inclusion of the
word 'well-being', which reintroduced non-medical considerations, and although it was incorporated at the committee stage,
Steel later agreed to drop it.

As the committee stage got under way a new virulent extra-
parliamentary opposition force—the Society for the Protection
of the Unborn Child—came into effective being. This belated
effort united a number of groups opposed to the Bill, especially
among Christian doctors and nurses, who as well as generally
opposing the Bill were urging the need for a conscience clause
lest they found themselves committed to perform operations
morally abhorrent to them. Such a clause was incorporated at
the committee stage. Parties sympathetic to the viewpoints of
the BMA and RCOG continued to plead in committee their
views on the status of doctors and hospitals, but their internal

divisions perhaps reduced their effectiveness and the Bill emerged from committee without amendment on this score.

The committee stage took so long that, the session being by now far advanced, there was a distinct possibility that the Bill would be unable to complete its final stages unless time over and above that normally allotted to private members' bills was granted. The gift of such time lay in the hands of the cabinet, and the unofficial Whips spent many man hours urging sympathetic MPs to lobby cabinet ministers for time. The matter seemed to hang in the balance, especially as the cabinet was not united behind the reform. The Prime Minister seemed to be both uncommitted and keenly aware of the significance of the Catholic vote in marginal constituencies. To strengthen his resolve, the opposition outside Parliament presented him with a petition of half a million signatures, many thousands of them from Roman Catholics, and the Society for the Protection of the Unborn Child was responsible for a spate of speeches and letters to press. The Abortion Law Reform Association retaliated with a massive postal assault on MPs and by publication of further opinion polls showing support for reform amongst the public and, importantly, GPs. A SPUC poll showed opposition to reform, but SPUC's counter moves came too late to dissipate the wealth of support garnered by ALRA.

The final stages in the Commons were a war of attrition, with the opponents of the Bill forcing debate at every juncture. Without the concession of time on two occasions by the government the Bill would never have passed through the House of Commons, but it eventually did and went forward for consideration by the House of Lords, which had already twice passed broadly similar Bills. Here the pressures of the BMA and RCOG secured a temporary victory in the shortlived deletion of the provision concerning 'children of the family' and also by the insertion of a provision requiring that the operation be approved by an NHS consultant or such a one as approved by

the Minister. The Ministry of Health, however, which had supported this view from its origin in the RCOG report of April
1966, had by July 1967 decided that it was unworkable, since
the small number of consultants appropriate (740) would produce an impossible bottleneck. It was not without vigorous
efforts by the ALRA lobbyists, however, that these amendments were reversed just in time for the Bill to complete its
passage within the session.

As well as the representations made by groups over the
wording of the Bills, the years 1965-7 saw vigorous publicity
campaigns by ALRA and, after January 1967, by SPUC. We
have already referred in passing to SPUC's petition and to
ALRA's use of commissioned opinion polls; in addition members of these groups attempted to influence opinion by all the
ways we have listed as being open to pressure groups. The
vigour of the ALRA campaign, which, partly through the
Association's greater experience and funds was the more professional of the two, cannot be overestimated. Its supporters,
numbering perhaps 2,000, were predominantly middle class,
female and non-religious.[10] SPUC, organised largely by
middle-class Christians and evangelicals, had only 300 members, but enjoyed much support among lay and medical
catholics and evangelicals. ALRA worked in close co-operation with the MPs who supported the Bill, and provided
facilities for the dispatch of hundreds of letters to other MPs,
keeping them informed of the Bill's progress and urging them
to vote. Also much personal lobbying was done throughout
by members of ALRA's voluntary executive. SPUC did not
play such a big role within Westminster, though its executive
kept in contact with leading parliamentary opponents of the
Bill.

In addition to the major groups concerned many others
signified support or opposition to the Bill through passing
resolutions or issuing statements. Abortion law reform was a

clear case of pressure groups having an influence, and perhaps represents the highwater mark of pressure-group intervention. But one must remember that it is relatively rare for groups to play so major and unrestrained a role as ALRA did.

Divorce Law Reform

This subject provides excellent examples of the different ways in which pressure groups become involved in the legislative process. As we have seen, in the 1940s and 1950s there were unsuccessful attempts to introduce divorce on the petition of the 'guilty party' after 7 years of separation from the 'innocent', but the divisions of the Report of the Royal Commission on Marriage and Divorce (1956) were symptomatic of the prevailing uncertainties on these questions.[11] The church's attitude to Leo Abse's attempt to introduce a 7 years' clause in 1962, however, provoked considerable adverse comment in the editorial columns of the popular press, and it seems likely that the general response to his Bill, combined with supportive noises from the Conservative government, was one of the factors that prompted the Archbishop of Canterbury in 1964 to set up a study group on the Church of England's attitude to divorce. Significant opinion was in any case changing, for although in 1963 the Lords had rejected the 7 years' clause, in 1966 the Divorce Law Reform Union found over 100 peers sympathetic to reform.

In 1966 the Archbishop's study group issued *Putting Asunder*, a report later accepted by the Church of England's Church Assembly. The study group recognised that there was a case for secular divorce, but felt that the sole grounds for divorce should be that the marriage had broken down. The existing matrimonial offences might constitute evidence of breakdown but should not constitute a *prima facie* case. Divorce by consent was no longer ruled out, provided the

F

marriage had broken down, and in the same way divorce on petition of the 'guilty' party (subject to safeguards for wives and children) became an explicit possibility. Each case, however, would be treated on its merits. The Labour government by then in office was sympathetic to reform but referred *Putting Asunder* to the officers of the Law Commission. These included Prof L. C. B. Gower, who 10 years before had unavailingly given evidence of his liberal views before the Royal Commission.

The Law Commission thought the procedure suggested in *Putting Asunder* altogether too cumbersome, and suggested that it would be more expeditious simply to add to the existing grounds, divorce by consent, after a specified number of years' separation, and divorce on petition of either party after perhaps 5 or 7 years' separation. There then followed several months of informal behind-the-scenes discussions between representatives of the Church of England, the Methodists, the Law Commission and the parliamentary reformers. Eventually they all accepted a suggestion put forward by the Lord Chancellor, Lord Gardiner,[12] which provided that irretrievable breakdown should be the sole ground for divorce, but that a matrimonial offence would be *prima facie* evidence of breakdown, as would separation for either a 2 or a 5 year period, depending on whether the suit was opposed. This formulation became the heart of the new divorce law.

Despite the Government's obvious and close involvement with the evolution of this Bill, it was still not formally adopted as government policy, and so it had to complete its passage within the limited time available for private members' Bills. Leo Abse was himself unsuccessful in the ballot of autumn 1967 but managed to persuade William Wilson to take the Bill, whose details were then finalised in discussion between Abse, Wilson and the parliamentary draftsmen.

In addition to the central provisions of grounds for divorce

there were now others concerning the rights to maintenance
of wives divorced against their will under the 5 years' separation clause. The Lord Chancellor and Leo Abse saw this as
the most vulnerable aspect of the Bill and were particularly
anxious to forestall the criticism that these wives, who had
'done no wrong', would suffer financially in that their ex-
husbands would be encouraged to remarry and deprive them
of their pension rights and probably, *de facto*, of their maintenance, too. They included in the Bill, therefore, the provision that in such cases the court had to be satisfied that the
financial settlement was 'reasonable and fair and the best
that can be made in the circumstances', and that if in the
opinion of the court the divorce would result in 'grave'
financial hardship, it could dismiss the petition. At that time
the government was reviewing the whole system of insurance
benefit, and probably hoped to come up with a more satisfactory alternative to the existing maintenance system; to specify
strict maintenance conditions in the Bill, therefore, would
have been unwise.

Shortly after it became known that William Wilson would
sponsor the Divorce Bill, he received a letter from Alastair
Service, a committee member of the Divorce Law Reform
Union, an organisation that was the not very active remainder
of the old Marriage Law Reform Society. Service had unusual
experience of the parliamentary scene, for he had been leading lobby organiser for the highly successful Abortion Law
Reform Association. Initially Wilson seems to have been
somewhat chary of accepting his offer of help, but soon
Service was, in combination with MPs such at Peter Jackson
and Sir George Sinclair, daily engaged in face-to-face discussions with other MPs in an effort to build up support for
the Bill. Many MPs expressed uncertainty about financial
provisions, and to counter this a small DLRU group, aided
informally by consultations with the Ministry of Pensions and

with the Law Commissioners, produced a leaflet outlining the existing provisions for the divorced wife. This was widely distributed among MPs and probably helped the reformist cause. Members of the DLRU executive also supplied MPs with facts and figures when it came to the detailed discussion of the Bill in committee, and the chairman of the Union endeavoured to maintain a favourable press coverage for reform. Also members of DLRU, many of them would-be divorcees, were enjoined to write to their MPs to impress on them the necessity for reform. This supportive campaign was sustained throughout the Wilson Bill of 1967-8, and after this had been killed by the end of the session, during the stages in both Commons and Lords of Alec Jones' subsequent Bill. The DLRU did not affect the content of the Bill, but the efforts of its officers and members contributed to its passage through the House.

During the spring of 1967 and subsequently, many organisations approached Mr Wilson. Some, like the Medical Women's Federation and the Salvation Army, had ideas they wished to have incorporated in the Bill, but many other organisations, including the Fawcett Society, the National Council of Women, the Open Door Council, the National Federation of Business and Professional Women's Clubs, the Catholic Parents Association, the Law Society, the Royal Medico-Psychological Association, the Probation and After-Care Service and the Society of Labour lawyers submitted memoranda on the Bill as it stood, suggesting detailed alterations or posing objections to particular points. Often their memoranda were passed to the Law Commission and the parliamentary draftsmen, whose unpersuaded rejoinders were transmitted back to the groups concerned. Many of the early communications expressed disquiet over the financial clauses, and William Wilson actually addressed a National Council of Women meeting to reassure them about such clauses.

Most of these groups seem either to have been satisfied by the replies they received or were not sufficiently concerned to press their points very far, for on the whole there was little further follow-up.

Sustained opposition to the Bill stemmed from unease over the vagueness of the financial provision for the wife divorced against her will, and from the religious objection that no person committed before God to a lifelong union should see this forcibly disrupted. On the first count the most vigorous extra-parliamentary efforts came probably from the Married Women's Association, which made representations to ministers, issued press statements and organised a petition of 12,000 signatures. The Bill's sponsors, however, were confident that the Law Commission and government would eventually produce regulations safeguarding the position of the married woman in divorce, and granted that the Divorce Act would not become law until these were operative, there seemed little point in making concessions on this issue. Further strong opposition came from the Mothers Union, which, with nearly 400,000 members, must have been one of the largest groups involved. It objected to the divorce after 5 years' clause in the following terms:

> Apart from the over-riding of any conscientious and religious objections of the 'innocent' partner, it . . . allows the defaulting spouse to benefit from wrongdoing, a principle hitherto unknown in English law.
> It would encourage the irresponsible husband, disillusioned with the domesticity of family life or bored by the middle-aged wife who having brought up his children, has lost her freshness and appeal, to form another attachment . . . It would leave the door wide open for the 'other woman' . . .

The Union also opposed the financial clauses as 'far from satisfactory'. Memoranda incorporating these views were circulated to MPs at three stages during the 2 years the Bill took to pass. In addition church dignitaries, including the Archbishop of Canterbury, realising that the new provisions had abandoned the thorough investigation proposed in *Putting Asunder* for the semi-automatic granting of petitions, pronounced against the Bill. The Baptist Union also took a stand in letters to MPs and members of the Standing Committee on the Bill, but the force of this opposition had been undermined by the church's initial acceptance of the substance of the measure. Inside Parliament the determined opponents of the Bill were largely sympathetic to the representations of these bodies, but the charge that they acted as their direct agents could never be sustained. The MPs followed their own initiatives and organised their own campaign, and it does not seem that the hostile extra-parliamentary lobby undertook any activities comparable to those of the DLRU.

The course of the Bill, however, went unexpectedly badly for the reformers. The text was long and complex and almost every clause and sub-clause was worth arguing about. The committee stage was lengthy and the parliamentary timetable by Easter so congested that there was little hope of the Bill completing its passage. Abse and his supporters, aided by the Divorce Law Reform Union, put considerable but unsuccessful pressure on the government to allow time. But the session ended, and there was nothing to do but begin all over again.

In the 1968-9 session Leo Abse secured the cooperation of Alec Jones, MP for Rhondda West, who had won ninth place in the ballot and persuaded the cabinet to allow time for the re-introduced Bill to complete its second reading. During this session the DLRU officers continued to support the passage of the Bill through unofficial whipping and circulars, and the Mothers Union continued to oppose by sending out its circulars all over again. Other groups, though watchful, were rather less active this time. Inside the committee in the House of

Commons the opposition fought a strong rearguard action, particularly on the financial provisions for divorced wives. Supporters of the Bill were confident that such wives would be catered for by the government's yet to be announced provisions, and opponents were convinced that it was immoral to take so serious a matter on trust. The Solicitor General attempted to reassure the committee on the point, declaring that no Divorce Act would come into operation until a Bill assuring the financial position of divorced parties had been passed. After a long struggle the Bill emerged from committee virtually unchanged, the reformers having had a comfortable majority. Its troubles, however, were not over. Recommitted, according to custom, to the floor of the House of Commons so that non-committee members could vote on amendments made in committee and add new ones, the first session was wholly absorbed by a move of Alec Jones, perhaps in response to pressures, to tighten in a modest way the clauses concerning financial hardship.

At several points thereafter the government had to give further time to enable the Bill to complete its passage as its opponents (dogged but not really well organised) forced one division after another, mostly in an endeavour to protect women already married. These attempts, however, were unsuccessful and the measure progressed to the Lords where one amendment, moved by Lord Reid, was incorporated, slightly restricting provisions for divorce after 2 years' separation.

The sponsors were at one time considering incorporating in the Bill the provision that litigants' solicitors should be obliged to bring to their notice the facilities of the Marriage Guidance Council, since the prevailing opinion was still that divorce was undesirable and must be averted wherever possible. But both the Law Society and the Marriage Guidance Council objected that such a stipulation would interfere with their relation with their clients. The Law Society sent a circular to members of the solicitors' group in the Commons asking them to oppose any such provision and the idea was dropped. So the complex Bill passed into law virtually as originally drafted by the parliamentary draftsmen.

Groups and Laws—a Complex Picture

These legislative attempts we have just studied show how difficult it is to generalise about the effect of pressure groups on Parliament since the volume of intervention varies from Bill to Bill. Without complete knowledge of all the Bills one cannot speak with certainty, but our own evidence, coupled with those of other studies of Parliament in action, suggest that the pressure-group activity surrounding the Medical Termination of Pregnancy Bills was out of the ordinary, both in its volume and effectiveness; that the group activity was small in the case of the Murder Bill; and that possibly the picture presented of pressure groups at work in divorce law reform is average. It must be remembered, however, that we have been concentrating on pressure groups, and may therefore have given too little prominence to the contribution of other participants, such as governments and MPs.

Notes to this chapter are on p171

5 Parliament's Role—What Influences It

We cannot accept Mrs. Whitehouse's generalisation that the Acts of Parliament sanctioning the permissive society were the direct consequence of the agitations of radical pressure groups. The Divorce Act began with the Church of England's *Putting Asunder,* but this was modified by the Law Commissioners and by Lord Gardiner. The Murder Bill emanated from Mr Silverman and Gerald Gardiner, members of National Campaign, whose parliamentary position enabled them to succeed where their groups had failed, but this Bill was modified by amendments introduced by Henry Brooke and by the Lord Chief Justice. The history of the Bill abolishing theatre censorship is not dissimilar. Former pressure-group leaders like Roy Jenkins and Noel Annan became members of the 1964 Labour government and House of Lords, and were thereby better able to pursue their pet subject, it is true, but a government committee was set up, and although church groups in their evidence seemed to support some degree of censorship, the representatives more immediately connected with the theatre, including the Lord Chamberlain himself, felt it was outmoded. The committee recommended abolition of the Lord Chamberlain's censorship powers and a private member's Bill to that effect passed into law with comparative ease. The

Sexual Offences Act legalised homosexual acts between consenting adults in private, but this had been recommended by church groups in evidence before the Wolfenden Committee 10 years before and was accepted and put forward by the Commons committee itself.[1] The Homosexual Law Reform Society campaigned for a Bill, but the Bill, when it came, was based closely on Wolfenden, with modifications introduced by Lord Dilhorne and Leo Abse and in minor matters by pressure from army and navy. None of the Bills would have become law without organised support from the Labour benches and from the Labour government. The Medical Termination of Pregnancy Act was, it is true, largely the product of group agitation, but groups applied only part of the pressures behind other Acts. Each Act was propelled by forces of its own, and one cannot generalise that this or that force was always predominant. There are, however, some recurrent features behind all of them—the government committee of enquiry, the strategic interventions of individual MPs and peers, the attitude of government, and the collective voting strength of MPs. It is the purpose of this chapter to examine these.

Government Committees

The role of the committee of enquiry has admittedly often been negative. The establishment of a committee blocks attempts at reform while the matter is *sub judice*, often for several years; divided or hostile committee reports often preclude prospects of success; and even unanimous recommendations have been ignored or overruled (eg, Wolfenden and Capital Punishment, 1957). Some committee reports have, however, formed the basis for legislation (eg, Wolfenden 10 years later).

Significant Individuals

Turning from committees to single persons, individual MPs

and peers have influenced Bills considerably with their ideas and beliefs. Take, for example, the interventions of certain peers in the Sexual Offences Bill. The crux of the Bill was the proposal that homosexual acts committed in private by consenting adults should no longer be offences. The opponents of the Bill, led by Lords Dilhorne, Kilmuir and Brockett, ensured that the definition of 'in private' would be more restrictive than that suggested by Wolfenden, not apparently because they were influenced by any organised backing, but seemingly because of a deep-rooted revulsion to homosexual practices and a determination that the new Act should not become a charter for mass orgies. A closely similar and ultimately successful Bill was later introduced in the Commons by Leo Abse, and the Homosexual Law Reform Society would have wished him to employ a looser definition of 'in private' and also to have lowered the age of adulthood from 21 to 18. Abse refused to yield on either count, however, partly because he was convinced that a more liberal Bill would not get through the House, and also because of his own belief that sexual orientations are not fixed at 18 and that the law should 'encourage' a youth to turn in heterosexual rather than homosexual directions. These seemingly personal interventions by Abse and by the peers are matched by the interventions of Gerald Gardiner in the the Divorce and Murder Bills, of Henry Brooke and Lord Parker in the Murder Bill, of Edward Lyons, who introduced a widening phrase in the committee stage of the Abortion Bill, and of David Steel and Lord Silkin in amending their Abortion Bills—all personal decisions.

Such interventions are often backed by expertise: Lord Parker's amendment to the Murder Bill carried special weight because of his position as Lord Chief Justice. Often they derive from practical exigencies; sponsors like Abse and Steel in shaping their Bills as they did had an eye to securing maximum support or minimum opposition within the Commons. Steel apparently amended his Bill because he doubted whether a more liberal text would secure a third reading. Abse, in the Bills he was most closely concerned with, consciously and deliberately attempted to phrase them in such a way as to disarm the main force of the opposition—hence the tightening of the definition of 'in private' in the Sexual Offences Bill and the inclusion of the financial clauses in the Divorce Bill.

It might be thought that MPs are merely bowing to organised pressure. Many of them in fact are associated with pressure groups of one sort or another. Apart from those we have already mentioned, Sir Lionel Heald and Mrs Jill Knight among the Conservatives, and Dame Edith Summerskill on the Labour side, were all associated with groups opposed to aspects of the Divorce Act, and Norman St John Stevas, who led the attack on the Medical Termination of Pregnancy Bill, was associated with the Society for the Protection of the Unborn Child. Such links are valuable for groups, since those that lack them, like the Voluntary Euthanasia Society, have little hope of promoting a successful Bill; but no group has any MP in its pocket, and even those MPs who are on the executive of pressure groups show a distinct tendency to act independently. Kenneth Robinson's relations with the Abortion Law Reform Association in 1961 are a typical example of an MP sympathising with a group yet keeping his distance from it. A study of the Clean Air Act describes a similarly delicate relation between the smoke-abatement group and Sir Gerald Nabarro;[2] Sidney Silverman, the abolitionist, also was hesitant about joining the National Campaign committee in case it hampered his operations within Westminster.

The extra-parliamentary group is entirely dependent on MPs and peers for its success, but the reverse is not true. Lord Gardiner and Mr Silverman were able to secure an abolition Bill without any external supporting campaign. Other MPs and peers make amendments which are not necessarily responses to external demands. Although they may have one eye on the House and one on the pressure group and electoral arena, any processes of taking interests into account are purely informal and rest on the judgment, right or wrong, of individuals as to how to pursue their aims effectively. MPs and peers can find themselves in a position to exercise considerable individual discretion. By deciding the wording of clauses and amendments they structure the decision for other people. By being present they are in a position to intervene and express sincerely held but personal opinions. Thus Lord Gardiner on becoming Lord Chancellor was able to give his blessing to the Murder Bill after 30 years' unsuccessful struggle for abolition outside Parliament.

The Role of Government

The contribution of commissions and individuals has been noted, but the major influence is that of government. Private members' Bills do not form part of the government's official programme, but even so governments become involved with them in various ways. In the first place the scope of government in this country is so large that any Bill is certain to impinge on some area of government responsibility—for instance, the Abortion Bill automatically involved the Ministry of Health and the Murder Bill the Home Office. In consequence sponsors discuss the relevant sections of their Bills with appropriate ministries. We saw in our case histories in Chapter 2 how ministries can effectively discourage attempts at legislation. Once a Bill has got under way ministries cannot stop it, but their support or opposition is a powerful influence. Ministers may persuade sponsors to withdraw a Bill they think would bring confusion in the law, a recent example being Ted Bishop's Matrimonial Property Bill. In other cases they may have doubts about particular clauses—the Home Office successfully advised against the rape clause in the Abortion Bill, and the armed services almost certainly instigated the exception of serving men from the provisions of the Sexual Offences Act. Ministerial pronouncements can help or hinder the prospects of a Bill: for instance, in the Abortion Bill the Minister of Health's initial acceptance of the Royal College of Obstetricians and Gynaecologists' position on consultants was a hindrance to the reformers, as was the Minister of Social Security's inability to be precise about maintenance allowances in respect of the Divorce Bill.

Governments accept a responsibility for seeing the technical workability of laws on the statute book, and so relevant ministries with their background squad of legal advisers are apt to point out where the wording of clauses is loose or of such ambiguity as would bring the law into confusion. It is difficult to draw the line here between purely technical advice and substantive intervention. The Sexual Offences Bill is the most obvious example of this process. The central clause of the Bill secured that acts between consenting adults in private should no longer be offences. Lord Arran's original definition of 'in private' was, however, owing to a technicality, replaced by a more restrictive definition proposed by Lord Dilhorne—'the commission of any such act when more than two persons are present shall not be deemed to be in private'—but later, after the Home Office had decided to offer drafting advice, the definition came out as 'done in the presence of persons other than parties to the Act or in a lavatory to which the public have ... access'. Obviously someone has to draft Bills, but he who does so occupies a position of power in that his words close some doors and open others. The parliamentary draftsmen were in the end responsible for drafting almost the whole of the Sexual Offences and Theatre Censorship Acts, and, of course, they were directly the authors of the Divorce Act.

Government's Role in the Passage of Acts

So far we have been principally concerned to demonstrate the political sectors which contribute to the content of moral laws. However, there is much more to an Act than its content. Bills can be produced easily enough but getting them through Parliament is a different matter. The normal procedure for a Bill is that after its introduction and formal first reading in either Lords or Commons it passes to a second reading debate at the end of which a vote is taken on its general principle. If that is approved, it passes to a committee, where it is examined in detail and voted on clause by clause, and amendments introduced. After this comes the report stage, at which the whole assembly, Lords or Commons, reviews the Bill in its new form and makes further amendments if it wishes. This stage is known as the third reading, and concludes with a vote, after which the Bill, if successful, moves to the other House, where it goes through the same stages and may collect further amendments.

A Bill can only succeed if an MP or peer is willing to sponsor it, and he or she must be ready, in addition to the normal workload, to negotiate with ministries and groups over the content of the Bill, and with the Commons officers over a suitable timetable, as well as undertaking to present the Bill to the public through the press and public meetings. Considerable energy must be devoted to building up and maintaining support amongst MPs and peers. A government ensures a majority vote for its policies by a system of official Whipping —checking and ensuring that sufficient MPs will be present at the right time—and those who ignore the Whip will be subject to informal sanctions and party discipline. For a private member's Bill, however, the sponsor must act as his own Whip. He cannot compel even those who are sympathetic to his Bill to vote for it, and since MPs and peers have many calls on their time, he has to work hard to muster support. Sponsors generally gather a small group of supporters willing to canvass other MPs or peers and act as unofficial Whips.

In the Commons the vote on the second reading is particularly significant, since the ratio of Ayes to Noes then is supposed to determine the proportion of supporters to opponents on the committee that considers the Bill at its next stage. A healthy second reading majority provides a healthy majority on committee, where again attendance is not compulsory and, given the many calls on MPs' time, a majority can be hard to maintain. At the report stage opponents typically table numerous amendments in the hope of defeating the Bill by absorbing all the time available for it. This tactic can only be beaten by moving to a vote as early as possible on each debated amendment, but in the Commons this can only be done if 100 members vote in favour of the closure. To safeguard a Bill at this stage, therefore, it is vital to muster a large number of supporters willing to stay all night if need be trooping in and out of the voting lobbies. The House of Lords is less embarrassed by these technical problems but presents its own difficulties in that their Lordships are, if anything, even less amenable to discipline than the Commons, and that for the radical reformer there is always the threat of the 700 hereditary peers, whose sentiments are usually assumed to be conservative, unexpectedly rallying in opposition.

The essential process of maintaining support for a Bill can best be accomplished by people working among those whom they know personally, and it has to be done by those with an intimate knowledge of procedure. A pressure group could not normally hope to accomplish this task successfully on its own, though the Abortion Law Reform Association came some way towards doing so. One of its members, Alastair Service, though not an MP, made full use of his constitutional rights to speak with MPs and peers, and in effect joined the band of unofficial Whips within the walls of Westminster. The association's Chairman, Vera Houghton, was similarly diligent, and ALRA, like the Homosexual Law Reform Society and the Divorce Law Reform Union with the Bills associated with their causes, handled much of the duplicating and addressing needed to deal with the perpetual streams of letters requesting and thanking people for support. However, a pressure group can never effectively control the passage of a Bill, and the canvassing work is usually done most effectively by MPs. Thus it is hard enough to get a private member's Bill launched and to sustain the vote for it, but there are also many procedural pitfalls which can ensnare it along its way. We have noted some in passing in our earlier case studies, and a narration of the difficulties that beset the Sexual Offences Bills will illustrate others.

Parliamentary Obstacles to Homosexual Law Reform[3]

In the early 1960s the vulnerability of the homosexual to blackmail was highlighted by a prosecution under the Official Secrets Act. Lord Arran in parliament remarked that had the government implemented the Wolfenden Report this type of risk would be diminished, but it was not until the advent of the Labour administration that there was real hope of reform. In 1965, in the early months of the new Parliament, Lord Arran introduced his Bill into the upper house. The second reading was highly successful, but omens were unfavourable in the Commons, where 2 days later Leo Abse sought leave to introduce a similar Bill under the Ten Minute Rule. He was formally opposed by a seasoned campaigner in Sir Cyril Osborne, who argued that the country needed sterner discipline not more licence. The Commons supported Sir Cyril, and leave to introduce the Bill was refused by 178 votes to 159. Thus the Commons, with its tiny Labour majority, was

G

not yet ready to vote for reform, a fact which Mr Abse ascribed to fear of constituency opinion coupled with the revulsion felt by many of the more traditional Labour MPs for homosexual practices.

Mr Abse's lack of success in the Commons did not impede the progress of Lord Arran's Bill, which embarked on a lengthy committee stage during which its details were thrashed out between Lord Arran and his opponents. Home Office views were also taken into account. This Bill, however, had been introduced too late in the session, in May 1965, and although it completed its passage through the Lords on 28 October, it simply had no time to get through the Commons in the same session of Parliament, which ended in October, and it was therefore lost. Lord Arran's time was not wasted in the sense that this 'dummy-run' provided an opportunity for the clarification of the Bill's wording, and the fact that it had passed once through the House of Lords without undue controversy probably facilitated its passage on subsequent occasions.

In the next session of parliament Lord Arran reintroduced his Bill, but before much progress could be made on it the Conservative MP Humphrey Berkeley, winning second place in the ballot for private members' Bills, decided to introduce an identical Bill in the House of Commons. This passed its second reading by 164 votes to 107, a swing in opinion as compared to the voting on Abse's Bill 9 months earlier perhaps to be accounted for by the success of Lord Arran's Bill, by the changing climate of opinion generally and by the fact that Berkeley was a Conservative and could claim some allegiance from his party (though Conservatives still voted 2 : 1 against the Bill). His success was fruitless, however, for his Bill, together with the rest of the legislative programme, was lost because the Labour government decided to go to the country in March 1966.

The general election produced a comfortable Labour majority, but despite the March start to the session there was no ballot for private members' time till the autumn. Lord Arran, free of such problems in the Lords, immediately decided to reintroduce his Bill, and it again completed its passage through the Upper House on 16 June. The Bill had now to go through the Commons and to guard against the notorious uncertainties of the ballot, its supporter, Leo Abse, started some characteristic manoeuvres. He decided to introduce a Bill of his own under the Ten Minute Rule, under which procedure members briefly introduce a Bill that can then be voted down or given a first reading. Normally it is just a publicity device, although it is formally a procedural alternative to the ballot. Bills introduced under it are only very rarely given time to proceed further; but in the case of the Sexual Offences Bill, as Abse's Bill was called, the government, it was rumoured, would make time available if a decisive majority voted for the measure, and the proportion of 244 Ayes to 100 Noes on 5 July, before the summer recess, was sufficient.

Throughout the summer Mr Abse worked hard to secure facilities for his measure, and ultimately the government intimated that time would be found for the House to reach a decision. He thereupon plunged into discussions with various parties on the wording of his Bill, in particular with representatives of the National Maritime Board, who felt that the Merchant Navy should be excluded from its provisions. Abse initially seemed dubious about this proposal, leading some of his opponents to believe that this sticky point, plus the exigencies of the timetable, would destroy the Bill; but to avoid defeat by the timetable, he managed to persuade ministers to nominate a separate standing committee to sit on his Bill, and then in committee accepted without demur an amendment exempting merchant seamen. The committee stage, in fact, lasted only one sitting, a dramatic comparison with the divorce and abortion Bills. Faced by the Bill's unexpected acceleration, the opposition attempted to block it in the usual way by tabling amendments during the report stage. These quickly exhausted the short time available for debate and the Bill would have been lost had not Abse again badgered the government into giving extra time. The Bill passed through the Commons after an all-night sitting during 3–4 July 1967, and its necessary passage through the Lords was free of all obstructions, so many times had it already made that journey.

Governments and Parliamentary Procedure

The history of the Sexual Offences Act demonstrates many of the pitfalls that can swallow up a private member's Bill. Lack of time is the main one. Bills have to pass through both Lords and Commons, and they can be blocked by the end of the session, by adverse votes, by prolonged committee or report stages, or by failing to find a sponsor in the other House. In the period 1965–9 the Murder Bill, the Medical Termination of Pregnancy Bill, the Sexual Offences Bill and the Divorce Bill all passed into law in forms not radically different from start to completion, showing that Parliament was favourably disposed towards them, yet in every case the reformers had to take more than one bite at the cherry.

According to our calculations there were sixteen attempts to pass these four Acts in this short period, a success rate of 25 per cent, if one assumes the final Acts were acceptable to the reformers. Only one of the Bills that failed was defeated in a vote—Leo Abse's Sexual Offences Bill in 1965. The rest were killed through lack of time or procedural difficulties. The House of Commons almost never finds time for Bills which start off in the Lords. No fewer than four Bills, two on abortion and two on homosexuality, passed through the Lords but were lost because there was no time for them in the Commons. Bills introduced in the Commons under the Ten Minute Rule, which are recognised to have little chance, can be stopped simply by opponents calling 'Object' at the time of the second reading, as happened to Mrs Renée Short's Abortion Bill in 1965. Two divorce Bills introduced this way foundered through the usual lack of time. As for the private members' ballot, the start to both abortion and homosexual law reform was delayed in the Commons because in the 1964 session no one lucky in the ballot was sufficiently interested in these topics. Ballot Bills with poor places can easily be talked out by determined opponents—the fate of Wingfield Digby's Abortion Bill in 1965. Even bills with good ballot places are not secure: William Wilson's Divorce Bill in 1967 did not finish its committee stage till so late in the session that no time was available for it to proceed, and Humphrey Berkeley's Sexual Offences Bill was lost when the general election supervened in 1966, an event which also stopped a Sexual Offences Bill introduced by Lord Arran.

Twelve Bills, therefore, failed to become law, though it was generally recognised from the outset that many of these attempts would inevitably fail. Their functions were partly propagandist and partly exploratory. However, when we come to look at the passage of the four successful Bills, we see that these too could quite easily have foundered had not the government, though officially neutral, intervened to save them. Opponents of Bills, be they a minority or a majority, have many constitutional delaying devices to prevent Bills completing their course, but these tactics, though actively employed against the four successful Bills, were foiled by government intervention. The government provided additional sessions for the Murder Bill when it was recalled to the floor of the House for its committee stage. The government twice gave the Abortion Bill extra time, and moved it to another committee to speed its passage. The Divorce Bill needed special help, as its sponsor had a low position in the ballot, and the government made time for it both during the early readings and at the report stage. The government encouraged Leo Abse to introduce his eventually successful Sexual Offences Bill under the Ten Minute Rule, allowed him a special committee, found him time for a report stage, and then, when lengthy debate prevented conclusion of that stage, gave him the extra time he needed.

The moral would seem to be that if a Bill is going to stir up even a small but reasonably concerted opposition, only government help can save it. By the government we mean ministers, particularly those of cabinet rank, and at least one or two of them must be sufficiently keen on a Bill to press its cause with the cabinet when it runs into difficulty. It is believed that Roy Jenkins and Richard Crossman were the ministers instrumental in persuading the cabinet that extra time be given for the Abortion Bill. Conversely, Richards has gone so far as to suggest that the failure of William Wilson's Divorce Bill to get extra time could be laid in part at the door of the Lord Chancellor as being less a persuasive advocate than some of the others.[4]

The Support of MPs

A final factor in the passage of an Act is the willingness of MPs to vote for it. The reform Acts we have mentioned were mostly passed on a minority vote, in that less than half the legislature took part in the divisions, but without these voters none of them would have become law. So what is it that makes MPs vote as they do? Do our guardians have guardians themselves?

We all like to believe that our judgments are our own, and that only the other man is biased. In fact, he is probably looking at the same facts as us from a different angle, but different viewpoints cause even reasonable men to disagree. What is interesting, therefore, is why people come to take different viewpoints. What are the influences, for instance, forming the guidelines for MPs? A host of factors are obviously involved—party line, immediate circumstances, public opinion, personal experience and general background. No one knows, however, which factor predominates in any particular MP at any particular time.

Party Line

Given that the British parliamentary system is one in which electors choose candidates who stand on party programmes, one could expect quite rightly that party policy would be an overriding determinant of an MP's parliamentary activity. On government business this is obviously so, the party in power and the party in opposition each securing their vote through the official Whipping system. But this conclusion does not take us very far, for it does not explain why and how parties come to produce different policies, and it overlooks the facts that party policy is often only a broad outline, whose details have to be linked by someone, and that there are some areas where there is no particular party line and ad hoc decisions have to be made. Further, it does not take us very far on the question of private members' Bills where the Whips are off and the voting is left to MPs' consciences. In the voting on private members' Bills on moral issues almost all the Ayes came from Labour and almost all the Noes from Conservative benches, but there were no official party lines on these issues, so why did MPs vote as they did?

Immediate Considerations

Sympathy for a cause is not enough: many MPs and peers have views on issues but do not record a vote thereon. This is particularly true in the House of Lords, where party discipline is less habitual than it is in the Commons. An analysis by Simms and Hindell of two consecutive divisions on the Abortion Bill in the Lords shows that 140 peers voted but only 57 of these were present at both divisions.[5] In the Commons, too, there is usually nothing like full attendance at divisions. Members have many valid calls upon their time, and since attendance during government business is more or less inescapable, private members' time is likely to be given a miss by those who are not zealots for a cause.

Here the efforts of the unofficial Whips are vital in cutting through the clamour of constituency meetings, fact-finding visits, surgeries, bazaars, business commitments and wives' birthdays. There is almost certainly horse-trading between the supporters of different bills—Jones will vote for Smith's if Smith will vote for Jones's. Some MPs will vote for a Bill because they owe the sponsor a favour. Obviously a minor element of chance enters into the matter, but it is the effort of the unofficial Whips that really makes the difference. Richards even suggests that the failure of the Sunday Observance reform was due to inadequate Whipping.[6] In the Acts which passed, the parties for reform were generally better organised than their opponents. Personalities, too, are important.

Constituency and Public Opinion

According to democratic ideology MPs should at least take into account the wishes of their constituents and the government should take note of the opinions of the electorate. There are, however, no systematic channels for doing this. The MP must rely on the feel of his constituency meetings, the leanings of the letters in his postbag and the editorials of his local press; and any pressure group on its toes endeavours to get its sector of the electorate to make its views apparent, especially via the letterbox. Occasionally constituency opinion is demonstrably important. In the summer of 1956 pressure from the constituency parties quite evidently caused certain Conservative MPs to abandon their policy of voting for the total abolition of capital punishment. It is also believed that in 1967 the Prime Minister, Harold Wilson, was hesitant about making time available for abortion law reform as this might have alienated Roman Catholic opinion in the marginal constituencies of the north-west. But it is not clear how much notice MPs take of the postbag and the constituency. Most probably they prefer to think that they make their own decisions, and only when they are undecided will a heavy postbag tip the balance. This does not mean that MPs are necessarily and frequently at odds with the views of their constituents, but simply that they do not want to be told what to do. In the main they will reach their own conclusions and make the not necessarily unfair assumption that those who elected them will be of like mind.

Similar considerations apply to the significance of 'Public Opinion'. Here it is interesting to contrast the history of abolition with that of other reforms. There can be no doubt whatsoever that the British public was opposed to the abolition of capital punishment: an opinion poll early in 1947 found 69 per cent in favour of the death penalty, and public hostility was certainly one of the factors that deterred the Home Secretary from including an abolition clause in the Criminal Justice Bill, as well as a factor influencing the Lords in their decision to reject the abolition amendment. Labour MPs, however, were far less responsive to such pressures, and a majority of those voting supported the amendment.

In 1956 the story repeated itself. Opinion polls showed that 79 per cent of the adult population was opposed to reform, yet most Labour MPs and now a substantial minority of Conservatives were prepared to vote for abolition. Again the Bill failed in the Lords, largely because the government was known to be opposed to it but in part also because of the well known public opposition. The government then, as we have seen, introduced the Homicide Act. The public apparently wanted total retention, and it is doubtful whether they welcomed the Homicide Act, with its degrees of murder, any more than they had wanted Sidney Silverman's Abolition Bill. From 1957 to 1962 reformers discreetly pressed the government to complete the process of abolition, and in 1961 they were particularly vigorous, but their efforts were counter-balanced by public clamour for the reintroduction of the penalty and a stiffer policy all round.

The government undoubtedly faced much backbench and constituency pressure for reintroduction at this juncture, but the Home Office, informed by the statistical results of its research unit, denied that the Homicide Act had led to an increase in the murder rate and stood out against reintroduction. Its strong line seems to have quelled the incipient constituency party revolt. On the other hand the Lord Chancellor in a Lords debate said amid cheers that it would be wrong at a time of 'so much public anxiety and concern about the prevalence of violent crime by young offenders to remove the sanction against the worst form of such crime, to which the vast majority of people . . . attach belief in its deterrent effect'. Popular opinion, therefore, was perhaps significant in averting further reform at this juncture, though neither the prime minister nor the majority of Conservative MPs were at that time abolitionists.

With the advent of the Labour government in 1964 all

such concerns were swept aside. Though even the most favourable public opinion poll showed 65 per cent opposed to reform, and though abolition was not mentioned in the election manifesto, the abolition Bill featured in the Queen's speech at the opening session and became law during that session, supported at its second reading by a massive 85 per cent of Labour members and 27 per cent of Conservatives. An amendment, introduced to limit the duration of the Act to a provisional 5 year period, moved by Henry (later Lord) Brooke, was certainly due to public opinion. In 1969 an opinion poll found that 83 per cent of respondents felt the penalty should be reintroduced for child murders and 78 per cent for the murder of a policeman.

The capital punishment case raises many interesting and, for the radical, perplexing, issues. Other reforms show a more straightforward pattern, in that they were effectively thwarted throughout the period 1935 to 1964. Ministers consistently refused to support them and even sympathetic MPs were pessimistic. Judging by the occasional polls, there was some support for divorce law reform, but after the inconclusive report of the Royal Commission this was ignored, and polls taken in 1963, when Leo Abse tried to introduce legislation, produced only weak support. The laws remained unchanged on this and other issues, though not explicitly because of public opinion, for we have found no record of polls on abortion or homosexuality in the early part of this period. The questions were simply not on the political map. In so far as the policy of the Conservative government and MPs reflected public opinion, it did so in a cocoon of mutual silence. Public opinion was, however, officially given as a reason for the government's non-implementation of Wolfenden's recommendation on homosexual law reform, and a poll taken after the report found under 50 per cent in favour of reform. Some influential members of the government were deeply opposed to this reform, but electoral considerations remained important, too, and continued to be so even with the Labour administration. In 1965 Leo Abse was outvoted in his attempt to bring in reform—a failure ascribed in part to fear of constituency opinion, interwoven with the repugnance of many older Labour members for the Bill.

However, the 1964 election seemed to radicals the likely harbinger of change, and after it the opinion polls proliferated. From 1964 to 1968 they showed growing support for reform on every issue except capital punishment.

The Abortion Law Reform Association was particularly alert to the possibilities of the poll, administering or commissioning at least four between 1964 and 1967. They sought the views of women, clergy and doctors and their encouraging results were brought to the attention of MPs and peers. The results of polls were also used by homosexual and divorce law reformers, though less vigorously. So far as one can judge from the polls a majority of the population in all social groups other than the Roman Catholics supported divorce, abortion and homosexual law reform. Support was strongest among the young and in the middle classes, and weakest among the over-55s and in the unskilled working class. One could argue that Conservative MPs who opposed reform were, therefore, out of line with both majority opinion and that of their middle-class supporters, and Labour members who supported reform were rather more enthusiastic than were their semi-skilled or unskilled electors. The reforms passed, with the exception of the abolition of capital punishment, can therefore be said to have enjoyed the support of the majority of adult Britons, though that is not to say that they were actually prompted by public demand. Public opinion just informed them and helped them on their way. The polls were taken only after an issue had already been mooted and often only when a reformist atmosphere was already developing in the mass media. Despite this, such polls were useful weapons in the armoury of the unofficial Whips, who could point out that an MP's constituents were at least not opposed to the reforms concerned.

In British politics the relationships between MP and constituency and peer and public are delicate. Propriety demands that a certain regard be paid to the wishes of the electorate yet the stronger tradition is of representative democracy. People are elected not to do the bidding of the electorate but to formulate programmes for it on the basis of their superior intelligence, political nous and grasp of the facts.

Personal Experience

Not infrequently the deepest held conviction springs from personal experiences or emotional impacts that leave a lasting scar. Thus Sidney Silverman attributed his long standing commitment to the abolitionist cause to his having heard of a partially blinded condemned man being scrupulously fitted by the prison service with a glass eye and then being taken out and executed—eye and all. The episode struck Mr Silverman as grotesque to the point of obscenity and was a formative influence behind his opposition to the death penalty. Similarly, Leo Abse has ascribed his concern over divorce, homosexuality and latterly adoption to situations coming to his notice in his legal work as a solicitor in Cardiff. Edward Lyons has attributed his feelings about abortion law reform to his wife being ill with German measles (which attacks the foetus) during pregnancy.

Pressure-group Propaganda

Small incidents produce a lifelong commitment, but they are probably potent forces for only a minority of MPs. Most form their opinions more at secondhand—from the advice of friends, from lectures, the mass media, books, documentaries, press articles, official statistics, and the broadsheets produced by pressure groups. A mound of information descends daily on an MP's desk. Much of it is destined for the wastepaper basket, but pressure-group handouts must have some effect, as does pressure-group canvassing of the uncommitted. There can be no doubt that the Abortion Law Reform Association built up its strength through dissemination of pamphlets and by individual lobbying.

The National Campaign for the Abolition of Capital Punishment in its heyday regularly plied MPs and peers with information, as did the Homosexual Law Reform Society. The Divorce Law Reform Union's pamphlet on the financial position of wives is believed to have quietened the fears of many MPs dubious about that aspect of the Divorce Bill. Some MPs are known to have had their opposition to abolition strengthened by the campaign conducted by representatives of the Police Federation. In these campaigns the radical groups were generally more professional in their propaganda, and in all probability more effective, than the institutionalised groups.

On the other hand MPs and peers tend to be sceptical of the influences of propagandist broadsheets; many were asked how far pressure groups had conditioned their opinions, and almost all rejected the very idea, sometimes in the strongest of terms. Yet surely, unless MPs are voting at random, such reactions are a little naive; their opinions must be influenced at least indirectly by the climate of opinion generated by pressure-group activity.

Background Factors

Some soils are more receptive to reformist plants than others.

We have often stressed that it was the coming to office of the
Labour government in 1964 which made reforms possible.
Several members of the cabinet were stoutly in favour of
them, and they were carried in the House by virtue of the
Labour vote. By contrast, in the years of Conservative rule
they were out of the question. It is not enough, however, to
attribute the change simply to innate differences between
Labour and Conservative, for the Labour administration of
1945 had the opportunity to introduce all these reforms and
failed to do so, not just because of its heavy legislative programme but also because there was a lack of support for them
among the Labour leaders, if not on the Labour benches.

In the 1950s Finer *et al* investigated the attitudes of MPs
on what they termed ideological issues—anti-colonialism,
the death penalty, etc—and on the 'bread and butter'
economic issues.[7] They found Labour members divided into
three groups—trade unionists; a miscellaneous group made
up of social workers, journalists and party workers; and
finally a group of men from the older professions. The first
group, though believers in radical change on economic issues,
held moderate or even right-wing views on ideological issues;
the second group were liberal in ideological matters but less
so over prices, wages and taxation; and the third group, of
older professionals, tended to be more middle of the road
than the first two on both counts. Between 1955 and 1966 the
trade union group diminished in numbers and influence within
the party hierarchy, while the second group probably increased in both. The composition of the Conservative Party in
Parliament was also changing. In 1955, though all sectors of
the party were 'right of centre' on ideological matters, the
graduates among the members, especially those from red-
brick universities, were less right-wing than the rest. By 1966
there had been a shift to the left on ideological issues among
all members. The coming to power of a new generation of

MPs with new ideas was a decisive influence in the success of the reforms of the 1960s.

A painstaking analysis by Fuller & Richards gives more detailed information as to which types of MP in the 1960s were the most ardent supporters and adversaries of reform.[8] To some extent different reforms drew on different resources. Abolition, for instance, had the support of the older ex-worker Labour MPs, but this group was less enthusiastic about the Sexual Offences Bill. The bulk of voters both for and against reform came from members of the professions, since these were the largest occupational group in Parliament. There were, however, differences among the major sources of support and opposition in terms of age and education. This we summarise in Table 1.

TABLE 1. LARGEST VOTING GROUP

Reform	For	Against
Abolition	Labour. State-educated, no higher education	Cons. Public school, Oxbridge
Sexual Offences	Labour. Under 45, state-educated, Oxbridge	Cons. Over 45, no higher education, or public school
Abortion	Labour. Under 45, state-educated	Cons. Over 45, public school
Divorce	Labour. State-educated	Cons. Public school, Oxbridge

Simplifying these differences we can say that the battle lay between the younger state-educated Labour members and the older public school Conservatives. If we could reduce the reformist and the reactionary to one MP on each side, the former would have most likely been a young Jewish or Free Church Liberal, state-educated and a professional man, and the latter a midde-aged (over 45) Conservative businessman educated at public school and Oxbridge. (One might substitute Labour for Liberal above, since there were so few Liberal MPs.)

On the whole these findings are not surprising. Few will be astonished to learn that state-educated Labour men supported reform or that public school Oxbridgeans opposed it. Yet to present the empirical findings is to pose a question rather than to answer one. What is it about the experience of the middle-aged and elderly upper classes that makes them relatively hostile to a liberal moral code? Theory suggests that men's attitudes and values are adopted and vary not according to some criterion of absolute truth but according to men's more or less accurate perceptions of their own life situations. The standards and attitudes passed on in family life and disseminated by cultural institutions such as schools, churches, the mass media, and pressure groups are combined to form a framework which makes sense of the world as it appears to be for most of us, and justifies the major activities of the economic and political systems of which we find ourselves part. Naturally, in a world open to new influences, new problems and sheer creativity, new ideas will constantly press to the fore, but those which conflict with the essence of the prevailing position will tend to be dismissed or misunderstood.

It would be pleasant to believe that no conspiracy is involved in the shaping of our ideas. Undoubtedly much of the time the common morality is passed on with a genuine belief in its self-evident rightness, but the history of fascism and communism clearly indicates that the group which controls the cultural institutions can propagate an ideology in which it believes and which presumably suits its own self-interests. According to vulgar Marxist theory, the capitalism which dominates contemporary Britain propagates an ideology that defends its own interests and dominates even those groups of society that stand to lose by it.[9]

H

True or false, in one way or another pressure groups are involved. Cultural groups such as the churches are important, either in their own right or else as disseminators of ruling-class ideology, and if we want to explain the radical position of the Labour benches, the formative influence of radical pressure groups must feature in the picture somewhere. The pressure groups that influence MPs in their formative years shape their subsequent voting behaviour, and we would suggest they are the most important single forces working for or against social change.

Thus in sum it seems that there are many influences other than the direct intervention of groups which affect the passage of legislation—the parliamentary timetable, the individual MP, and the disposition of the government and of the ruling party. Pressure-group activity affects these things, too, but indirectly and through a long-range viewfinder.

Notes to this chapter are on p171

6 The Influence of Groups Reconsidered

We are now in a position to answer the questions and speak to the fears raised in Chapter 1. That chapter began with the assumption that lawmaking in a complex society was the business of the political elite—to the possible exclusion of the mass of the populace. But there are, as we saw, those political theorists who believe that the operations of pressure groups are one of the safeguards of democracy, and, consequently, that pressure groups play an essential part in the political system. After our investigations of lawmaking on moral issues we are better able to evaluate these claims, and we shall do that first. But we also noted in Chapter 1 the criticisms of pressure-group theory that only a few groups participate in lawmaking and that some of those which do, particularly those representing dominant economic interests, wield disproportionate influence. In the latter part of this chapter we shall consider these criticisms.

The weight of evidence suggests that government and Parliament exercise a decisive control over the business of lawmaking and that the role of pressure groups is at best indirect, at worst negligible.

The clearest example of pressure-group intervention came in abortion law reform. The role of the Abortion Law Reform

Association was probably everything a group could wish for. By providing the Bill itself, ALRA set the terms around which other groups had to argue, and despite concessions on some points the Act incorporated a large slice of its programme. No other group had quite the same success, though the interventions of the British Medical Association and the Royal College of Obstetricians and Gynaecologists were obviously almost as important. The cooperation of the medical profession was vitally necessary if the Act was to be workable, and it is clear that the views of the medical groups carried weight with the sponsors and with some of the government departments. The importance attached by members and sponsors to the pronouncements of the Church of England on divorce, abortion and homosexuality is worth noting, but blatant intervention by pressure groups was not a feature of the other pieces of legislation to which we directed our attention.

Groups may besiege a citadel, but its walls can only be stormed within Parliament and by parliamentarians. As legislation gets under way, groups tend to become mere spectators unable to control the process of drafting, debating and voting. They may, though, and frequently do, make an effective contribution to the administrative side of getting a Bill through by providing secretarial facilities for the sponsor, lobbying MPs and by supplying any necessary statistics. ALRA and the National Campaign for the Abolition of Capital Punishment were particularly strong in these services. Groups further disseminate general propaganda among MPs and peers and organise constituents into writing letters at appropriate moments. It is generally acknowledged that without this sort of industry Bills could not muster sufficient voting support, though if sponsors do not want groups to help in this way, they are precluded from doing so.

Another aspect of the supporting campaign is the press and publicity drive which a group may be able to provide while a Bill is going through Parliament. Press articles, public meetings and opinion polls can help to maintain a sympathetic climate. ALRA and the Homosexual Law Reform Society both exploited this tactic, as did, to a lesser degree, the Divorce Law Reform Union.

The successful campaign often means an unsuccessful defence, like those of the Society for the Protection of the Unborn Child (abortion), the Mothers Union (divorce) and the Police Federation (capital punishment). Of course, without the presence of opposing pressure groups the reforms might have been even more radical: for instance, the potential hostility of the women's organisations over the financial provisions of the Divorce Act was certainly taken into account by the sponsors.

Groups also contribute to the legislative process by taking sponsors up on matters which affect group interests. Often this amounts to little more than a polite exchange of letters, but sometimes, as with the Law Society's intervention in the Divorce Act, it can lead to a change in some point of detail.

All this refers to the interventions groups make in the immediate business of lawmaking, and from it one must conclude that those interventions are generally of a restricted character. However, the business of making laws is not exclusively confined to the passage of a Bill. There must first be a demand for a Bill, the forming of a suitable climate of opinion. It is here, arguably, that groups make their major contribution. Campaigns like that mounted by the HLRS between 1958 and 1965 or that of ALRA from 1963 onwards made people rethink their attitudes towards homosexuality and abortion. These groups' activities stimulated wider and more liberal coverage of the issues in the mass media, and though it would be a mistake to imagine that every working man in Wolverhampton became a champion of, or even interested in, abortion law reform, these vigorous campaigners cultivated a public climate in which reform was possible. Their pamphlets also reached MPs, and if the ground was already receptive these pamphlets must have had some confirmatory influence. The final decisions and wordings lie with the parliamentarians, but on the whole there is a feeling that parliamentary Acts should embody public opinion.

We have observed, too, how in the build up to an Act of Parliament a government committee of enquiry frequently plays a historical role. Sometimes the activities of pressure groups (divorce, capital punishment) were instrumental in establishing these committees, but even where they were not, groups generally seem to have looked on the setting up of committees as likely to lead to victory. Hundreds of groups give evidence to such committees, thus taking part in the political process; and one can see the impact of church, police and medical groups, largely directed towards preventing reform. Group power to prevent reform is also a positive contribution to pluralism.

Groups do not always manage to contribute to the legislative process through this channel, since group views have to be mediated by the commissioners themselves. In a perfect world interested parties could put their plaints to genuine neutrals, but, though the composition of a committee is a matter of great delicacy, the outcome must always be biased. Either factions are systematically represented and the report divided or more usually an attempt is made to discover the mythical neutrals. There are genuine degrees of open-mindedness, and people do in fact change their minds while sitting on committees (the conversion to abolition of Sir Ernest Gowers, chairman of the 1957 Capital Punishment Commission is a good example), but no living man is truly neutral—he must necessarily bear the markings of his upbringing and profession. Commissioners are usually recruited from the upper strata or more recently from 'established' trade unionists. Some pressure groups thus have an additional influence in so far as they are part of the world-picture of the commission. More directly though, the evidence groups give has to go through the uncertain sieve of the minds of the commissioners, and it is the commissioners and their opinions that command attention rather than the evidence submitted by groups.

Another problem with commissions is that, even where group opinion is judiciously weighed by the commissioners and a near unanimous report emerges, it can be ignored by the government, as was the Wolfenden Report, or be overruled, as were certain findings of the 1957 Capital Punishment Commission. So, though groups have on occasion participated in the legislative process by this means, it is an uncertain and indirect channel for them.

The views of government are decisive, but even here groups are not entirely without influence. As we have argued, MPs and peers are not moral neutrals. Their views are necessarily drawn from the intellectual currents of the era to which they belong, and groups are major generators of those currents, not just in their immediate campaigns but also through their brief pamphlets and ill attended meetings. They are agencies disseminating opinions which, impinging on the consciousness, become imperceptibly part of the taken-for-granted world. This indirect and uncertain process is the most common, perhaps the most important and certainly the most insidious form of group intervention in the political field. It is too uncertain and indirect a method to satisfy the pro-pluralists, however, and too sinister and uncontrolled for the anti-pluralists.

So groups do play a role. They give evidence to committees, they stimulate public opinion, and they educate by campaigns while Bills are in the offing and more generally over a period of years; yet when all is said and done their contributions tend to be confined to the periphery—to the supportive campaign, negotiations over details, the watching brief or ineffective huffing and puffing. It cannot be said that every reform Bill receives effective contributions from even two or three groups. The Abortion Bill was an exception. The Divorce Act found the Church of England fairly directly involved, but the interventions of other groups were largely monitory, or weak and ineffective. In the Sexual Offences and Murder Bills the most important group contributions were indirect—the opposition of the police over the years, the sterling work of the National Council in converting left-wing opinion in the 1920s, and the efforts of the Homosexual Law Reform Society to create a climate favourable to change. When it came to the Bills themselves, neither of these groups nor any others were able to do anything effective, despite their willingness to help.

Our examples have been drawn largely from three moral law reform Bills, but we do not believe that our conclusions are too untypical. Had we looked at the struggle for reform of laws on obscenity, Sunday observance, euthanasia, suicide or illegitimacy, the general picture would have been much the same. At best one could talk of muffled or surreptitious pluralism. Groups are involved to different degrees, and generalisation is difficult, but it does seem fair to say that (1) on moral issues the small campaigning groups make little or no headway against a hostile government, (2) that no group can promulgate an Act at will, (3) that groups do not dictate a Bill's content and they cannot guarantee its passage, and (4) that establishment groups held sway in early years not so much through their own efforts as by virtue of their general identification with the status quo, and later they were unable to prevent reforms.

Groups cannot be called the saviours of democracy, especially when one considers the allegations of unfairness critics like Wolff have levelled against group activity or lack of it. How many groups are involved in issues concerning them? An examination of the available case histories shows that on some issues a wide range of groups were active, but on others almost none; in no case we examined did we find that all the groups concerned with an issue took some action.

Take, for instance, the abolition of capital punishment. It will be remembered that an NOP poll conducted in November 1964 indicated that 65.5 per cent of the electorate were in favour of the retention of capital punishment, and only 21.3 per cent thought it should be abolished. However, the Bill which virtually abolished capital punishment provoked hardly any response at all. In 1969 an ORC poll found 83 per cent in favour of the death penalty for those who murder children, yet there was little sign of any parents' group opposing the Bill in 1964. No trade unions, apart from police and prison officers' representatives, and no shopkeepers, most of whose members were presumably opposed to the Bill, expressed any opposition, particularly surprising perhaps in the case of bank clerks and jewellers, whose jobs might be supposed to leave them particularly vulnerable to the armed robber. Neither do there seem to have been any concerted representations from imprisoned murderers, from the relatives of executed murderers or the relatives of victims, all of whom might have been presumed to have specially relevant experience. For good or ill most interested groups were silent.

Similarly, in divorce law reform, women (or men) most likely to suffer financially in divorce were poorly represented in so far as they had no separate organisation, and although the Mothers Union and others purported to speak for them, it is not clear that the potential sufferers played any major role in framing the policy statements. In any case these groups had little direct impact on the shaping of the Act.

Even where the major contestants do appear to be fairly represented it is always possible to think of other potentially interested groups which fail to make an entry. Almost any Bill would demonstrate this, but the abortion case is particularly interesting to explore because superficially it appears to be alive with group activity. Obviously the Abortion Law Reform Association provided the spearhead of aggression for this Bill and the medical associations and the unsuccessful Society for the Protection of the Unborn Child the bulwark of opposition. However, there are many groups to whom the abortion question is of interest. Some religious groups made their opinions known but the smaller churches apparently did not, nor did other groups—fathers, persons with congenital deformities, adoption societies, childless families, baby food manufacturers, nurses and midwives, and overcrowded families all come to mind. It would seem, therefore, that many subsections of the population never put forward their views on issues apparently of concern to them.

It is possible to argue that opinion on any Bill can really be crystallised into a crude choice of for or against, so that all the pro-abortion factions found a home in groups like ALRA and all the opposition in groups like SPUC. This argument, if it is to be accepted as an example of the working of democracy, would first have to be true; secondly, it would break down unless the sub-interests all obtained adequate representation within the umbrella groups; and thirdly, it would have to be demonstrated that the larger groups were actually listened to by MPs. So it is not difficult to show that the sceptics have a case in arguing that in the negotiations over any political issue some groups go unrepresented.

Given the small range of groups involved and also the fact, noted in Chapter 3, that active groups are scarcely mass democratic organisations, one might conclude that the tight control exercised by the political elite is a safeguard rather than a hindrance to democracy. But how far is the elite itself free from the influence of a minority? Do capitalist economic interests dominate all areas of our life?

In Chapter 2 we described the joyless morality that covered the official face of Britain in earlier years. Its code on matters of life and death, sex and modesty was directed towards maintaining the integrity of the family, and projecting the monogamous union as the sole expression of sexuality. Fear of promiscuity and perversion was reflected in the laws against abortion and homosexuality, in the condemnation of adultery, in the divorce law, the propriety of the natural order on birth and death, and in attitudes to contraception, abortion and euthanasia. The standards set by these laws were felt to protect the sanctity of family life, and confirm the rightful status of woman as dependent on her husband (reflected in the divorce law maintenance provisions) and as a child-bearer; she had to be defended outside marriage by strict tabus and encouraged within marriage by laws against abortion. Inextricably interwoven within these central dispositions was a whole set of taken-for-granted arrangements about the care and protection of children and the elderly, and a web of financial dependencies —pension rights, property law, rights to medical services, etc —which it would be unwise to disturb. This code, as we have said already, was underpinned by the virtues of self-control and a consequential punitive attitude towards defaulters.

We have no doubt that these views were ingrained in the majority of the pre-war populace, and passed on in some measure to their children. They were reflected in, and fed by, the discreet attitude of the mass media, including the attitude of Lord Reith's BBC to sexual matters and by the attitudes overtly sustained by welfare workers, doctors, magistrates and other authority figures, especially schoolteachers, who as part of everyone's common experience must have been paramount in the transmission of attitudes. So general were these ideas that for most part there was little need for open defence of the status quo, but on occasions when established mores seemed threatened, there were groups sufficiently concerned to come forward. These presumably were the bulwarks of the old morality. Thus the British Medical Association in 1936 tried to shelve the report of Bourne's working party as paving the way for a surge of irresponsible demands for abortion. Their caution over contraception, let alone abortion, has already been noted. In the 1950s the Roman Catholics were the most outspoken opponents of abortion law reform, but it is clear from the eventual stand of the BMA that doctors had not modified their views. The established church also opposed reform.

Church groups provided the major voice, too, in opposition to radical reform of the divorce law in the 1950s.[1] Marriage was a sacrament, a vehicle of God's grace—and indissoluble. The existing system of divorce after matrimonial offence was, however, accepted as a regrettable necessity.

Opposition to reform came also from the leading groups of the legal profession. Like the Church of England, the Bar Council put forward several objections to divorce after 7 years' separation, principally that no one should be able to profit from his own wrongdoing and that no 'innocent' wife should be divorced against her will. It also saw little need to introduce divorce by consent. Educational groups such as the Association of Headmistresses and the National Union of Teachers felt on balance that divorce had worse effects on children than the friction of quarrelling parents.

It was not the church groups that opposed homosexual law reform. Submissions from the Church of England, the Catholic Union and other groups positively advocated reform and their recommendations were largely accepted by the Wolfenden Committee.[2] Reading between the lines of the report, one can see that the police, however, were not enthusiastic about changes, but it is not clear where their opposition to this reform lay, other than in an automatic repugnance that most males seem to feel for homosexual behaviour.

As to the death penalty, we have made it clear that belief in its justice and deterrent effect was deeply engraved in British mores. To many it was seen as essential to the preservation of the weak, such as women and children, and to others essential as a defence against the armed criminal. The Police Federation consistently expressed the view that in the absence of the penalty robbers would not hesitate to use weapons, and there is little doubt that this was an influential argument in official circles, though over time members of the police forces became less unanimous on the point. The church's spokesman to the 1948 Commission did not object to the continued use of the penalty.

One could say, therefore, that in the period up to 1963 the most successful pressure groups in matters of moral concern were the churches, the medical associations, the established lawyers and the police, since the opinions propagated by these groups won acceptance both from the Royal Commissioners and more importantly from government. These groups did not go about issuing prophetic calls to man the barricades, but rather represented the articulate tip of an iceberg of opinion. Whether this opinion was universal throughout society is another matter. What is important for now is that it controlled most of the middle class and the leadership of society, including MPs and peers of all parties.

Why did opinion change? Some of the more imaginative and perceptive brains of our age have suggested that it was due to the force of economic necessity.[3] They argue that the hard work, self-discipline, ploughing back of profits and generally postponing gratification necessary for the early capitalist entrepreneur, and still necessary for the independent businessman and the aspirant white-collar worker, could only be achieved by a type of personality in whom sexuality was heavily repressed. Hence the oppression and joyless morality. By the second half of the twentieth century, however, the capitalist economic system has come to need not disciplined entrepreneurs and obedient producers but flexible and spend-thrift consumers. For the system to survive it is now necessary for the repressed personality to be replaced by one more liberal —one in which sexuality is symptomatically liberated. At the same time the new found sexuality is pressed into the service of the economy via advertising, and in a whole industry aimed at sexual titillation. According to this thesis the basis of morals had to change because it had become an obstacle to the economic interests on which we all depend. If this is true, it leads to the interesting conclusion that Mrs Whitehouse, with her stand for traditional values, is doing more to destroy the capitalist system than left-wing MPs like Abse and Jackson.

Mills and Miliband take less determinist positions, simply pointing out how the relative wealth of the owners of industry not only means that they effectively dominate large areas of our lives—income, costs, available products—but also that they are in a position to 'out-propagandise' any move contrary to their interests.[4] The upshot is that economic interests form the dominant pressure groups in society. They may operate at several levels—directly, through intervention in the political system by passing new laws; indirectly, through 'agents'; or simply by acquiescing in changes made by others that are consonant with their own purposes.

This theory has a superficial plausibility and maybe contains a grain of truth, but no more than a grain. In many ways the consumer boom fits well with the ethos of the permissive society, but there was no organised businessmen's lobby in favour of reforms, it would be absurd to suggest that the journalists who wrote articles favouring them were deliberately furthering capitalist interests, and even more absurd to attribute such intentions to the leaders of the radical pressure groups. Such groups as the Ethical Union and the Marriage Law Reform Society, for instance, had no financial backing other than subscriptions from a few thousand members, most of whom probably considered themselves to be anti-system anyway. We have already explained that we consider these groups were significant in disseminating over a long period reformist views which became orthodoxies for many Labour politicians, and we cannot but believe that they exercised their influence independently of economic pressures. They were, of course assisted by other forces. Especially important was the gentle shift in opinion of the established church towards a more liberal position over divorce and abortion, and its unmistakable call for reform of laws governing homosexuality and capital punishment. Was this capitalism's undercover agent at work? It is argued by Miliband and others that the established church, though no longer the Tory party at prayer, will still endorse state, and *ergo*, business interests.[5] However if in this case the church was the agent of the capitalist class, it was surely unwittingly so.

Materialism, secularism and business motives may have had something to do with the changing climate of opinion, but these influences were independently predated and paralleled by those of the radical groups and the new style Church of England. Also many of the events that symbolise the period of change—television satire, Thalidomide, pop music, *Look Back in Anger*, women's education, sociological research— have little connection with capitalist economies. The suggestion that businessmen were directly involved in the passing of reform Bills cannot be sustained either. In fact, an analysis of several votes shows that they were the group most consistently hostile to the reforms. The Ayes were the new-style Labour politicians.

While it is hard to attribute these reforms to the purposeful machinations of the capitalists, one could, of course, argue that the developing economic system necessitated widespread education and ultimately generated a new elite that undermined the old system; but in this version the conspiratorial argument loses most of its force.

The final argument in the theory that economic interests

were the force behind reform—that the capitalist class simply acquiesced in reforms which would benefit it—is difficult to sustain, since in many ways the reforms are at variance with economic interests. The cult of women's liberation, though good for the economy in some senses, is at root a threat to the sale of beauty products and of products for the home and family around which any consumer boom must be oriented. Similarly, personal liberation for women and homosexuals could in later years develop into a demand for liberation from other taskmasters and for self-determination in other spheres. No entrepreneur can have any realistic hope of weighing all these odds, and it is unlikely that the entrepreneurial group in any sense calculated that it would be better to permit these reforms than to suppress them. I think we have to admit that the economic picture presented by Miliband is not complete. We have to modify the opinion we expressed in the first sentence of Chapter 5, and admit that Mrs Whitehouse has some justification in blaming pressure groups for setting the scene for reformist legislation, but she may or may not be relieved to know that the progressive liberalism of the Church of England was also an important contributor.

Notes to this chapter are on p172

7 *From Particular to General*

The first six chapters of this book were a self-contained whole in which the problem of pluralism was posed and examined in connection with the law on moral issues. Such law is but a small fraction, however, of the whole programme of legislation and administration conducted at Westminster. What is the role of groups on other types of issue? In this chapter we want to see how far the conclusions reached earlier are valid for British pressure groups in general. It may be best to begin by restating our findings on the role of groups concerned with moral issues.

Moral Pressure Groups—Conclusions

We divide them into two categories—the first composed of large groups, well institutionalised in the social structure, either purporting to represent legitimatised sectional interests, like the BMA, or cultural organisations, like the church groups; and the second comprising radical pressure groups, which were almost all small and non-bureaucratic, and run by small committees with effectively no responsibility to anyone. During the 1950s the radical groups directed their campaigns (1) towards the public, through leaflets and meetings, and (2)

129

J

towards Parliament, by lobbying MPs and the government through pamphlets, letters, petitions and deputations.

These campaigns, allied with intra-parliamentary pressures, succeeded in persuading the government to institute wide-ranging committees of enquiry, the net effect of which was to quash hopes of reform. During the late 1950s even sympathetic MPs and peers were discouraging, and the institutionalised groups favouring the status quo did not need to campaign very vigorously to maintain their position. But matters changed in the early 1960s, when campaigns mounted in intensity, and through a complex of forces support for the reforms multiplied and led to legislative enactment by the Labour administrators of the later 1960s. Pressure groups had little to do with the content of Bills, except on the abortion issue; otherwise their role was confined to indirect or marginal intervention. The Bills other than the Abortion Bill in fact were shaped variously by the Law Commissions, the Wolfenden Committee and by the personal interventions of particular members of the legislature. Admittedly the Bills were generally along lines long urged by radical pressure groups, but all were dependent for their passage upon the vigorous action of particular MPs and peers, on marshalled voting strength and upon significant help from the government of the day. The view that economic interests dominated was at best doubtful. Radical pressure groups played some role in forming the climate of opinion among MPs and the country at large, while their opponents, the institutionalised groups, either capitulated or campaigned ineffectively against reform.

Summarising these conclusions we would say that (1) campaigns by radical groups have no hope of success while the government is hostile; (2) even when unsuccessful they may be performing a useful role in keeping alive support among the opposition; (3) conservative groups can maintain their position, given a favourable government, with relatively little effort; (4) groups have little direct effect upon the content of legislation, though their ideas may find their way independently into it; (5) groups can do little to ensure the passage of a contentious Act, which is dependent upon the good offices of the government; (6) groups opposed to reform can do relatively little in the face of a determined government; and (7) pressure groups may indirectly influence reform in so far as their ideas inform the basic predispositions of the government.

Now let us consider how far do these conclusions carry over into other areas of government. The evidence is at once copious and inadequate. Case studies similar to our own document the struggle over voluntary euthanasia, birth control,[1] nuclear disarmament,[2] equal pay,[3] reform of drug laws and trade union legislation,[4] and the passage of particular Acts such as the Television Act 1954,[5] the Clean Air Act 1956,[6] the Commonwealth Immigrants Act 1968,[7] the Race Relations Act 1965,[8] the Monopolies and Restrictive Trade Practices Act 1957,[9] the Rent Act 1957,[10] the Theatre Censorship Act 1965[11] and the Housing Finance Act 1972. There have also been occasional studies involving not Acts but policy formation and administration, notably those on the genesis of the health service,[12] farming policy,[13] national insurance,[14] and defence policy.[15] In addition to these case studies there are several general books on pressure-group activity that provide brief examples to illustrate their themes.[16] The range of material, therefore, seems encyclopaedic, but in fact many areas of life are still not included, and even the available information is not always sufficiently complete to permit of a full comparative analysis.

The studies just mentioned differ in many ways from those mentioned earlier in this book. There are struggles on a variety of issues at various times—for and against Bills, over private members' and government Bills, and over governmental administrative decisions. We propose to dwell on only a few major themes—the experience of campaigning groups, the process

of administration, and the role of groups in government
legislation.

Similarity of Campaigns

Among the case studies are several that describe a campaigning history—subjects include euthanasia, nuclear disarmament,
drugs, smoke control, race relations, equal pay and birth control—and one is struck by the similarities in the methods used.
On the one hand there is always the public campaign, with
leaflets, press articles, sponsored news stories, advertisements
and books—tactics used by groups as disparate as the National
Federation of Property Owners pushing for rent decontrol in
the 1950s and the birth-control movement of the 1930s. Public
meetings and meetings under group auspices also form part of
the campaign. Occasionally dramatic tactics are employed.
Petitions or marches, such as those of the Campaign for
Nuclear Disarmament, Vietnam Solidarity, or against the Industrial Relations Act, have become increasingly frequent and
now have all the inevitability of the public meeting of earlier
years. Dramatic gestures such as the break-ins, sit-downs and
fastings of the anti-nuclear Committee of One Hundred have
been infrequent.

The more important side of the campaigns is the pressure
put on MPs and the government. Again, pamphlets are in-
variably sent and strenuous efforts made to secure the assistance of MPs or peers willing to press the government through
parliamentary questions or by introducing doomed Bills. The
birth-control campaign and the Voluntary Euthanasia Society,
CND and the equal-pay campaigns certainly used these tactics.
The picture is always the same—aid from an MP personally
committed to a cause in loose alliance with a group, perhaps
letting it sharpen his ideas but ultimately asking his own questions on his own rather than the group's behalf. The Birth

Control League and CND, like the National Campaign for the Abolition of the Death Penalty, tried to build up support within the Labour Party, hoping to persuade its national conference to pass resolutions that would then become incorporated in party policy. The tactics of sponsoring MPs or running independent candidates was used by CND and by the anti-Common Market campaign, but is not very common.

It is widely argued by political commentators that this type of campaigning, directed towards a non-specific public and in a somewhat hit or miss fashion at Parliament, is almost always unsuccessful—witness the struggles of the CND campaign, the VES, and the legalisation of 'pot' movement, as well, of course, as the experiences over many years of the Abortion Law Reform Association and other groups we have already dealt with. It is clear from the evidence that governments are reluctant to get involved with certain issues, be it birth control or conservation. It may not be that governments are actively hostile on these matters, but they simply give them indefinitely low priority. Even on matters on which the government takes a stand, there will be groups whose viewpoints are unpopular and unacceptable—unilateral disarmament, for instance. Any extreme group will have to endure long years in the wilderness—writing unread pamphlets, persuading MPs to introduce futile bills, sending fruitless deputations to ministers. The early histories of the birth-control, CND, smoke-campaign and euthanasia movements all run along these lines.

Many of the case studies, of course, have happy endings, but this should not mislead one into feeling that in the end a breakthrough must inevitably occur, for there are hundreds of groups (I'm Backing Britain, the anti-breathalyser campaign, anti-vivisection) which campaign unsuccessfully, and maybe ad infinitum. Since they are unsuccessful, their histories tend to go unrecorded. It is even possible that a majority of campaigns end in failure, though failure is relative. It seems possible that just as the abortion law reformers and others were formative influences in the creation of opinion, so too the birth-control groups, the equal-pay campaigners and the smoke-abaters succeeded in differing degrees in shaping ideas, and sometimes, though there is no easy recipe for saying when, a confluence of circumstances culminates in a change of attitude and a change of policy.

The programmes advanced by the birth-control movement, by the equal-pay campaigners and by those variously advocating control of atmospheric pollution and laws against racial discrimination were in the end all met to some degree. In each case the role of organised interest groups was only one factor at work. There were also important precipitating events, like the great London smog, which killed 4,000 in 1952 and played a great part in the introduction of smoke-free zones, and the electoral consequences of the women's vote, which is believed to have affected the government's equal-pay policy.

Nor were groups completely alone; they were often independently supported by internal parliamentary forces of some significance. There were abortive attempts via the private members' Bill procedure on both clean air and race relations. The history of the smoke-control issue is strikingly similar to that of the moral reform groups.[17] The National Smoke Abatement Society campaigned in the usual style with the usual lack of success until the abovementioned fog of 1952 prompted the government to establish the Beaver Committee on Air Pollution. This committee's report accepted many of the NSAS's proposals, and soon Sir Gerald Nabarro was attempting to introduce a private member's Bill, whose story was the not unfamiliar one of uneasy compromise between groups and sponsors, and eventual loss because of an election (1955).

Pressure Groups and Public Administration

Many of the operations of government do not involve law-making. In truth one might say that the bulk of civil service time is not spent in forming laws at all but in administering laws already made. In view of this the paucity of evidence on the role of groups in the administrative process is striking indeed. It is generally admitted that as government becomes involved in wider spheres of national life, it cannot conduct its policies without close working relations with the relevant pressure groups, both because it needs the benefits of their expert advice in order to formulate intelligent policies and their active cooperation in order to carry them out. Government is directly responsible for a great many areas, such as health, roads, nationalised industries, and is indirectly involved in numerous other activities, so constant month by month if not day by day consultations are necessary with the parties concerned. People get to know each other in this way and the existing joint committee system provides opportunities for the raising of new ideas and the improving of former methods. Governments can consult groups about incipient changes, and groups can advise civil servants about the best way to deal with problems that might arise. Groups also have regular contacts among MPs which they use especially when governments seem dilatory or indifferent.

One special device that brings Whitehall and interest groups together is the consultative committee.[18] In 1954 there were 484 such bodies attached to the various government departments, ranging from the Grassland Utilisation Committee, the Standing Dental Advisory Committee, and the Probation Advisory and Training Board to the Joint Advisory Committee on Foundry Goggles. These committees are made up of civil service representatives and representatives of interested outside bodies. They meet for general discussions and exchange

ideas on matters of concern. Governments can use them as a
sounding board for new policy initiatives, and the interest
groups can press their views in return. The author J. D.
Stewart, writing on the role of pressure groups, seems to
emphasise the significance of the advisory committee,[19] giving
several examples of groups using the committee to induce
ministers to change minor matters—for instance, in 1950 the
drapers persuaded the Joint Committee on Retail Margins for
Apparels and Textiles to remove certain price controls.

However, there are in practice effective limitations on the
powers of consultative committees. Their role is generally only
advisory, and ministers can and do ignore their advice. A
study by Political and Economic Planning declares that the
consultative committee's influence 'is admittedly nebulous and
is sometimes alleged to be negligible. Those who look for
definite results and decisions from the work of consultative
committees will not find them; but to do so is to mistake their
function.'[20] Their function it seems is the airing of views.
Committees do not dictate policy. The process of consultation
is one in which government retains its superior position, exer-
cising discretion as to just how sensitive to be to group
opinion; though some committees may exercise considerable
influence because the technical expertise of their members
leaves little room for discussion.

One would not dispute the value of consultative committees
despite the difficulty of exactly evaluating their significance.
At the same time they do not cover all areas of life. There are
councils for some industries but none for others, manufacture is better represented than distribution or consumption,
and, furthermore, the interest groups invited to send representatives are almost always the legitimate and institutionalised
bodies.

Occasionally negotiations break down. The government for
its own reasons may refuse to accommodate the group's posi-

tion. Groups then may resort to campaigning tactics, generally again with poor chances of success. The case studies, though few in number, seem to bear this out. The two best known record (1) the cooperation between the Ministry of Agriculture and the National Farmers Union, and (2) between the Ministry of Health and the British Medical Association over the setting up of the health service. The NFU was able to work very closely with the Ministry, both under Labour and Conservative governments, possibly because governments of either persuasion seem keen on retaining the farming vote.[21] Another study, of the relation between the Ministry of Defence and the armed service chiefs, tells the story of a breakdown in the late 1950s after the unsuccessful Suez invasion when the Conservative government determined to cut the cost of military spending, opted for a policy of nuclear deterrence, and instituted changes without the heartfelt agreement of service chiefs.[22] This led to the unusual spectacle of senior service personnel acting like other pressure groups and declaring their views through the press and public speeches.

Groups and Government Legislation

Government legislation grows up against a general background of which the committee system is one factor. Other factors, perhaps more influential, are party policy and departmental folklore. In areas where the government has undertaken an enduring responsibility for administration the civil servants and the ministers in charge develop a mental construction of the situation which conditions what they will do. Certain problems and solutions present themselves. It is generally agreed that governments retain control, and in fact the case studies lead one to the conclusion that the group role in policy formation is practically nil.

The accounts of the monopoly law and laws on housing and

clean air leave one hazy as to the forces that provoked the Bills. They seem to have been the culmination of a long chain of events, beginning with problems inherited from previous governments, and pushed on by committees of enquiry whose uncomfortable findings could not be ignored by the Conservative administration owing to some ill defined notion of public and press opinion. The Monopolies Bill, for instance, emerged because the reports of the Monopolies Commission set up under the Labour government indicated the widespread nature of certain restrictive practices[23] whose existence and detriment to the public good were confirmed in the commission's mind by a special and wide-ranging enquiry, despite representations from industry to the contrary. The commission recommended prohibitive legislation. The government was not enthusiastic and both main political parties were divided on the issue, but apparently the chance coincidence of court cases and bad press publicity pushed the Board of Trade into framing legislative proposals. There is no evidence of pressure groups angling for the reform other than an unconfirmed suggestion that local authorities may have been irritated by restrictive practices. It is worth noting, however, that the National Smoke Abatement Society had three members on the Beaver Committee on Air Pollution, whose recommendations formed, though through a long-range viewfinder, the basis of the Clear Air Act. In that case the role of the pressure group was more evident than usual, though it was still only one factor among several.

The Race Relations Act of 1965 also arose from an assortment of sources.[24] Several MPs had been pressing for legislation for many years, and two or three groups of left-wing MPs and lawyers had drafted possible legislation before the election of Labour in 1964. The activists on this occasion were members of the Labour intelligentsia rather than pressure groups in the usual sense of that word, though they did manage to convert to their scheme the Campaign Against Racial Discrimination and its member bodies, which subsequently lobbied vigorously for the Bill; but as usual the significance of pressure from MPs shows up as decisive. The Commonwealth Immigrants Bill and the Television Bill illustrated this pressure even more significantly. The Immigrants Bill of 1968 was a rush measure by the Labour government to prevent an influx of Kenyan Asians who, like the Ugandan Asians of 1972, were being displaced from their homeland.[25] In his account of the Bill's passage, David Steel does not make it entirely clear why the government felt the measure to be necessary, but the picture emerges of a Labour government stampeded by pressure from right-wing Conservative MPs who, through press and parliamentary campaigns, painted a picture of a Britain more black than white. The introduction of commercial television, like the Immigrants Act, is generally attributed to the operations of a small group of determined Conservative MPs who converted a hostile or indifferent Conservative cabinet from automatically giving its allegiance to the BBC into desiring an independent medium financed by advertising.[26] In these two cases there were no effective formally organised pressure groups, though at the more implicit level the commercial TV lobby had an obvious umbilical relation to industrial forces.

These case studies are picturesque but not necessarily typical: indeed, they tend to be written up precisely because they are special. Our accounts of the passing of the Commonwealth Immigrants Act and the Television Act were intended to demonstrate the vulnerability of Parliament to attacks from within, and one should not conclude that legislation is typically introduced in this way. The Race Relations, Monopolies and Rent Bills probably represent the more usual course of events. The conclusion suggested is that groups do not play a big role in the genesis of government legislation.

The study of private members' Bills forced us to conclude that groups only rarely participate directly in writing in the details of legislative proposals, an experience apparently repeated for government bills. J. D. Stewart writes: 'It is only in very unusual circumstances that the actual draft of a bill will be discussed between the department and the group.'[27] This view is on the whole borne out by the case studies. The original Bills on Immigration, Clean Air, Race Relations and Rent were drafted in the ministries, with more or less knowledge of the views of groups but with no direct attempt to consult them. There is an unconfirmed suggestion, however, that the leader of the Association of Land and Property Owners, formerly a civil servant, exercised some influence on the ideas incorporated in the Rent Bill.[28] On commercial television and monopolies there is evidence of rather more direct intervention. Without the pro-commercial lobby's strenuous efforts the commercial service would probably not have started at all, but the hostility of the National Television Council, a typical campaigning group formed to fight the proposal, probably prevented the adoption of a straightforward sponsorship system and made sure that the new service would not be financed exclusively from advertising revenue. The influence of these groups was therefore important, though the drafting of the provisions in these Bills was done behind closed doors.

We have already described the early history of the Monopolies Bill. After the Monopolies Commission had produced its suggestion for legislation a series of statements were produced by the large manufacturing and retailing organisations, and consultations did take place between these groups and the Board of Trade. Almost certainly this resulted in the ministry's decision to choose, the Commission notwithstanding, a judicial rather than an advisory committee to rule on infringements of the new law. But this was a solution that also suited the ministry, and on other matters the groups were not at that time successful. Thus there may be seen to be a continuum of consultative practice ranging from an apparent zero in the case of the Immigrants Bill to the more obvious intervention over monopolies and commercial television. Unfortunately the evidence is not sufficiently accurate or comprehensive for one to decide how much consultation is general.

In the study of private members' Bills we categorised the many and various efforts of groups to influence Bills once they have been published by pressing matters with the sponsors and inducing sympathetic MPs to move amendments. A closely similar pattern emerges in respect of government Bills. Again a relatively rich source of data comes from J. D. Stewart, who gives numerous examples of groups intervening, especially in the committee stage, to amend detailed points in legislation.[29] He describes, for example, how the Association of British Chambers of Commerce was partially successful in amending the Budget; how the National Union of Manufacturers obtained some sort of satisfaction on the matter of estate duty in the 1953 Finance Bill; and how NALGO (National Association of Local Government Officers) successfully intervened in the Transport and Housing Bills, but was less fortunate over the Electricity Bill.

The case studies demonstrate the varying degrees to which groups manage to bring in amendments during the passage of a Bill. On the Commonwealth Immigrants Bill they achieved virtually nothing, since the Bill was rushed through in something like 4 days with only one minor amendment. The extra-parliamentary opposition to the Bill had little time to organise, and although it was actively supported inside the House by many MPs, interventions were unsuccessful once the government had made up its mind.

The Race Relations Bill was intended to penalise instances of racial discrimination in public places, and incitement to racial hatred.[30] Its original draft made these criminal offences, but after a stormy outcry and much lobbying from both right and left, it was conceded that discrimination in public places should be classified as a civil offence. This might be represented as a victory for the Campaign Against Racial Discrimination and for the pressure applied by those individuals who had urged this position. But on the other hand the Bill did not go so far as the pressure groups wanted on several important points, and Keith Hindell, author of the case study, implies that the government, having then only a tiny majority and anxious to secure a smooth passage for the Bill, softened its provisions and let it be known that in view of the crowded timetable it was virtually this Bill or nothing. In fact the Bill was so phrased that support from the Conservative benches facilitated its passage, overruling Labour dissidents.

The Bill that introduced commercial television was, as we have already said, the product of several years of pressure from MPs with the interests of the industrialists at heart.[31] By the later stages of the campaign favourable powers in the Conservative hierarchy added the material and practical support of the Conservative Central Office to the commercial lobby, though sections of the party still opposed the Bill. Its opponents were a belatedly organised agglomeration of educational, cultural and business interests (film producers). During the Bill's passage the government went some way towards meeting the complaints of both supporters and opponents of the Bill on points of detail: the powers of advertisers were restricted in various minor ways, and so were the powers of the newly created overseeing authority and the Post Office. On the Monopolies Bill also the manufacturing and retailing confederations were eventually able to secure some concessions, though not all they would have liked.[32]

In respect of the Bills on Rent and Smoke Abatement the evidence available is less clear. Malcolm Barnett says that the National Federation of Property Owners secured two 'relatively controversial' amendments to the Rent Bill,[33] and it is clear that the NFPO and the National Smoke Abatement Society found MPs and peers willing to press points and secure some amendments, though again these did not disturb the major principles of the Bills.[34] Once again the dependence of groups on MPs and peers willing to take up their cause was to be emphasised.

It is difficult to generalise because some groups did apparently gain concessions. On the other hand, some groups, having had their case rebuffed, seem simply to have shrugged their shoulders; while groups which cared passionately, as did the opposition to the Commonwealth Immigrants Bill, were unable to prevail despite recourse to the tactics of the public campaign. Stewart gives several examples of groups resorting to such campaigns after they had failed to prevail with the ministry.[35] He records some successes, but his general opinion confirms our own that groups which have failed to impress the government or to gain support among its members are unlikely to convince it through campaigning tactics. Governments, it seems, have the final say.

In summary, genuinely extra-parliamentary groups like the Abortion Law Reform Association occasionally manage to get a Bill through Parliament, or sub-groups within Parliament like the commercial TV lobby occasionally manage to influence the mind of government. Many groups have an institutionalised stake in the process in the shape of consultative committees, but this does not enable them to control the content of legislation. Groups rarely command the drafting stages of a Bill, but they may, if sufficiently persistent and if they have good parliamentary contacts, manage to amend it, as did the Labour group on race relations and the industrial groups over monopolies, though even these did not secure everything they wanted. Other groups, like the

National Smoke Abatement Society and the National Federation of Property Owners, secured minor amendments. Many groups get nowhere, just shouting from the sidelines, holding a watching brief, or, like the pro-immigrant lobby, failing totally. Most authors of case studies seem to feel that, in the end, groups play only a limited role.

Given this general situation, are some groups consistently exerting more influence than others? One thing is certain: as with the moral issue Bills, only a few of the potential groups are apparently actively involved with government Bills. For instance, all sorts of groups might logically be expected to have had an interest in the Immigrants Bill—immigrant groups themselves, international friendship associations and trading interests, constituency opinion, and those responsible for education, health, or housing—but all those were hardly consulted or ignored. We need not labour the point in such detail for other Bills; it is sufficient to remark on the weak representation of tenants with regard to the Rent Bill, of consumers to the Monopolies Bill, of heavy industry to the Smoke Abatement Bill, of actors and technicians to the Commercial TV Bill, and of the National Front to the Race Relations Bill.

The Power of Big Business

The evidence from the case studies superficially supports the contention that economically powerful groups exert a predominant influence on legislation. Table 2 may provide a handy reference point.

We have arranged Table 2 with the issues in roughly descending order of overt pressure-group activity. The case studies of commercial television and monopolies do suggest that the forces of industry are powerful and persuasive, and that once pitted against them those same cultural groups which enjoyed relative success over moral issues would be the

TABLE 2. GROUPS PRINCIPALLY INVOLVED
most successful in bold type

Issue	For	Against	Unorganised
Commercial TV	**Popular TV Assn** (Manufacturers & advertisers)	Nat Broadcasting Council (educ & cultural groups)	Viewers
Monopolies	? Local Authorities	**CBI & NUM**	Consumers
Race Relations	CARD	?	Right-wing groups
Clean Air	Nat Smoke Abatement Soc (members incl industrial groups)	Industrial interests	
Rent Decontrol	Landlords	Tenants	Unions Tenants
Immigration	?	NavaKala (an immigrants' association)	Right-wing organisations

losers. The Television Act is usually seen as specially significant, for bringing advertising into the living room was a
master-move on behalf of consumer capitalism. More spending and more personal possessions keep the wheels of industry
turning, and higher living standards result, especially for the
upper classes.

On clean air and rent decontrol the impact of big business
is less obvious. One should remember, however, that industrial groups such as the National Coal Board and other
industrial groups were affiliated to the National Smoke Abatement Society, and that the government's Bill was rather
weaker and consequently more favourable to heavy industry
than NSAS had wanted. As to rent decontrol, it has been
suggested that the representatives of ALPO (the Association
of Land and Property Owners) may have exerted some influence over details of the Bill, but the evidence is not very
decisive. What emerges more subtly from Barnett's account

K

is the way in which the Bill was almost unconsciously framed within the prevailing norms of capitalist ideology: since there was a housing problem, the obvious solution was to move towards a free market in dwellings and make it economically attractive to the private landlord to improve his property.

These case studies can be used to support the view that the powers of capitalism tend to dominate on economic matters. To them we might add the passage of the 1971 Industrial Relations Act and the 1972 Housing Finance Act, both of which serve the upper classes rather better than the working man. But these studies are not necessarily conclusive. For one thing, the economic interests of the larger companies were better served than those of the smaller in the Bills on commercial TV and rents (though the position was reversed in the Monopolies Bill). For another, the Bills were not entirely hostile to the interests of labour: the Rent Act should have improved homes by facilitating repairs, the Monopolies Bill curbed monopoly and commercial television improved viewing. Furthermore, before accepting the case-study evidence as conclusive, one must remember that most of these Bills were enacted during a period of Conservative government, and Conservative support for the interests of capital will surprise only the working-class Tory. Indeed, one might say that the government was simply carrying through its mandate from the electorate. It would be more instructive to analyse the role of capital in the 1964-70 period of Labour government. David Steel has suggested that expanding business interests prevented the Labour government from putting pressure on the Kenyan government at the time of the expulsion of the Asians.[36] But this view is just plausible speculation and, though it may corroborate Miliband's thesis that the capitalist class dominates, it is not decisive evidence.

Notes to this chapter are on p172

8 *What of the Future?*

The usual reason for examining the entrails of the dead is to predict something about the living. We have seen something of the life-style of a small selection of pressure groups of the 1950s and 1960s. Have we presented an accurate picture of the role of groups in British political life? Certainly we feel confident as regards the case studies on moral issues, and while the possibility remains that there are other types of group/government relation which have not come to light, the evidence shows a certain unanimity as to the typical experiences of the small campaigning group, and as to the forms of group intervention in the political process and the checks thereon.

The campaigning groups saw much of what they had asked for translated into law by the Labour administration of the latter 1960s. At the time the changes seemed to many tantamount to the licensing of a perpetual Roman orgy, yet by the cool light of 1972 the reforms were fairly modest. There is still no abortion on demand, and control over legal abortion lies firmly in the hands of the medical profession, rather than in the hands of women; homosexuals remain circumscribed in their public displays of affection and in facilities for securing partners by restrictions that would be outrageous for the heterosexual; divorce, even by 'mutual consent' remains a protracted business, taking over fifty times as long as it takes to get married. Many causes dear to the radical conscience— Sunday observance, drugs, euthanasia—could still be fought to a conclusion. The campaigning groups would still appear to have a function left, and in the 1970s we see them being joined by groups standing for new causes such as conservation, pupil power, prisoner power, patient power, etc, all completely unthinkable 10 years ago. Another new development is the resurgence of groups like Mrs Whitehouse's National Viewers' & Listeners' Association or the Festival of Light, formed to defend the traditional values of religion and purity. In the past the orthodox could depend on their values being defended by institutionalised groups such as the Church, the Conservative Party, social workers, teachers, etc, without having to think about the matter, but in the current world none of these agencies is wholly reliable.

To left and right, therefore, groups are showing activity. But will their experiences be similar to those encountered by the groups of the 1950s and 1960s? This is a difficult question. We do not know whether groups always tend to take the same paths, or whether group behaviour can be amended by the actions of creative human beings. The latter seems a distinct possibility. One evident characteristic of groups today is a tendency to reject the old idea of working through Parliament for a change in the law, and to turn instead to forms of direct action and self-help. Organisations like Shelter, or the de-schooling groups, spend less time on attempting to change housing policies or the 1944 Education Act than on trying to create a living alternative. All the same, even direct-action groups come swiftly up against the powers of government, and given the extending network of laws and regulations in all areas of our lives, a strategy for confronting the lawmakers will always be necessary.

Another new feature on the contemporary scene is a militancy and violence more conspicuous than that which characterised protest movements of the 1950s. There is a return to a form of protest buried during the immediate post-war years—that of the mass rally, increasingly feasible in the days of motorways and relative affluence, but increasingly boring and developing a traditional end in violence. The trend could be accounted for in many ways. A study of civil rights movements in the USA concluded that in the early days of the movement the low status and education of blacks left control of the movement in the hands of a small group from the professional class, who worked for reform through legal channels; but as blacks became more self-directing and assumed greater control, the movement turned increasingly towards more militant tactics.[1] The British story may prove to be similar. Certainly the reformist movements of the 1950s and 1960s were dominated by professionals working in a liberal, humanist, Fabian tradition which basically did not question legal means and the rule of law. It would be absurd to claim that revolutionary radicals did not exist in the 1950s, and equally unrealistic to maintain that they form anything like a majority in contemporary movements, but remembering that ALRA, the DLRU, and the NCACP in the 1950s confined themselves to the petition, the pamphlet and the public meeting, one must allow that current trends are more flamboyant. Whether they are *ipso facto* more successful we shall consider in a moment.

One reason why our discoveries about the past are not directly relevant today is that the experiences of groups then were the product of specific historical circumstances. The campaigning groups worked and struggled against the odds for 10 years or more before reform came, but there is no law in history which says that this must be so. Obviously their experience was circumscribed by the fact that the Conservative government, in power for 13 years, was hostile to these reforms. Furthermore the traditions of the period meant that governments were then less attuned than they are today to the idea of forming their policies on the basis of evidence now supplied by groups. In that era, as the evidence to commissions shows, both groups and governments tended to work on hunches. Today the approach is more statistical, and that may increase departmental reliance on group resources. We have noted, too, the role played by Royal Commissions, but again they have no necessary role in our future history, for future governments might abandon them.

There are then several notes of caution for anyone who would hope to extrapolate with certainty from the experience and success of ALRA to his own movement of the future. All the same we do not believe that the study of history is idle amusement. In many respects the system does not change. The basic parliamentary system remains, with its private members' Bill procedure (despite the fact that every commentator suggests modifications), and the law remains; and a great many groups still seek to change the law in much the same way as did NCADP 50 years ago. We believe that they will enact many scenes similar to those already enacted, that they will campaign in vain, that their routes to direct intervention in the political process will be cut off, and that their best ideas will be taken over by government and MPs. We believe further that groups will continue to play an inevitable but indirect role in the forming of opinions. Ought the role of groups to be strengthened? Before examining the difficulties and philosophical pros and cons of such a solution it is only fair to draw attention to a few of the arguments in favour of leaving the system as it is.

An argument powerful in some quarters is that to increase grassroots intervention in political life would increase public inefficiency. The administrative effort of ensuring that every possible group was consulted would be unbearable, and the resulting chaos of views could be calamitous. Furthermore, the views from the grassroots would frequently be at odds with the more reasoned views of the experts. Capital punishment is a pertinent illustration. Most people conversant with the technical evidence came to believe in the wrongness of the death penalty, yet public opinion remained solidly behind it. Further, the anti-pluralists have always argued that groups are detrimental to democracy and equity because, representing sectional interests, they take no thought for others, and, since some groups are by nature better endowed than others, a system which gives pride of place to groups is one that institutionalises inequality. Only a strong government, it is said, can take a broad view and enact laws for the national good, and such a government is necessary to restrain the power of sectional interest. This argument can be proposed by right or left, by Mills or Whitehouse, on the grounds that some objectionable groups override the general good.

On this sort of basis one might argue that the role of groups is already too strong or that at best the existing system by which government and MPs manage through various devices to keep pressure groups at arm's length provides a balance of the best of all possible worlds. The conventions surrounding advisory committees, and the independent status of MPs, ensure that the parliamentarians can step back and put pressure-group opinion into the wider context of the national interest and the electoral mandate.

It is also worth reminding oneself that the health of democracy does not rest on pressure-group representation alone. An MP is in touch with his constituency through letters and weekly 'surgeries', he reads the papers and the opinion polls, he even talks to taxi-drivers. More importantly he is himself a member of society elected by people whose views are presumably much the same as his. If he feels a certain way on an issue, it is not unreasonable to suppose that his electors will feel that way also.

These are powerful arguments, from which one might conclude that any talk of increasing the role of interest groups is either superfluous or dangerous. We would suggest, however, that there are effective counter arguments.

In the first place it is not realistic to rely on MPs automatically knowing the views of their constituents. MPs do not form a representative sample of the populace, being predominantly male, well educated non-manual workers, and even the scars of a working-class childhood fade away when one rises to a position of relative affluence. Certainly no MPs can really be in tune with the multiplicity of relevant interest-group opinion. It was argued that MPs keep in touch with the public mind via opinion polls and the letters in their postbag, but these are surely unreliable means. A study of the American system by Bauer indicates that letters from constituents are often ambiguous and unwittingly misinterpreted.[2] Furthermore, in the British system only certain groups are sufficiently alert to mobilise their members to write to MPs at appropriate times, and under these conditions pressure on the postbag verges on manipulation.

As to opinion polls, we have already argued that their role is indirect and confirmatory rather than a conspicuous spur to legislation, and many objections could be lodged against their being anything other than an approximate rough guide to actual feelings. Various problems arise when a citizen with no particular interest in divorce is asked out of the blue: 'Are you in favour of or opposed to the suggestion that *either* partner should be able to obtain a divorce after 7 years' separation?' Firstly, if he is not really very interested in divorce, the poll with its bald yes/no categories will certainly disguise the fact. Secondly, if asked the question out of the blue, the answer may not coincide with what the respondent would feel if he came face to face with the situation. Thirdly, the seemingly simple question about divorce by either party after 7 years' separation conceals complex issues about the doctrine of matrimonial offence, and they would possibly not be sufficiently familiar to the average respondent without further explanation. Take a question on abortion. 'Should a woman be able to have an abortion if the baby was likely to be born seriously deformed?' Although 91 per cent of women answered 'Yes' to this question, we do not really know what they meant by seriously deformed. Some may have had Thalidomide babies in mind; others may have confined their definition to anencephalic children. The House of Lords spent many hours arguing about the definition, ending their debate by deciding that the definition should be highly restrictive—but there is no reliable evidence that this accorded with the wish of the general public.

Polls, of course, aim to establish the facts about what people think. The polls commissioned by the Abortion Law Reform Association always used clear-cut non-emotive questions like the example above. The Society for the Protection of the Unborn Child, however, using questions couched in much more emotive language, also secured support for its position, though the response rate was poor. It was probably easier to give a quick definite answer to the ALRA questions because they were more clearly phrased, but this does not automatically make those answers more reliable. It is well known that the form of the question inevitably biases the response. We are not maligning anyone who uses polls as part of their campaign, since they are at least attempting honestly to get at public opinion. We only wish to enter a note of caution about the interpretation of the answers, and to stress that they do not provide a very secure foundation for the representatives of that opinion to base their policies on. Anyway poll and postbag are irregular and unsystematic forms of communication.

The arguments in favour of bolstering group intervention are that, first, each group is expert in its own field and thus has information conducive to efficient policy-making; and second, that people have, if not an obligation, at least a right to conduct their own lives and to try and influence events according to their opinions. Finally, it is no use relying on the just hand of a benevolent government to dispose all things well for us, for, as we argued in an earlier chapter, there are no neutrals. All have biased vision and they develop their biases very substantially through the process of direct or indirect exposure to the influence of pressure groups of one sort or another—from the implicit emphasis of schoolteachers on competition or discipline, to parents, with their experience of trade unions and bosses, heartbreak and love. In this indirect sense the influence of groups in social life is ineradicable, and for this reason maybe we should be more concerned about who it is within these groups—unions, churches, professions, consumers, mass media—that generates the ideas which indoctrinate us.

In the rest of this chapter we shall consider ways and means by which the significance of groups in the political process might be augmented. We shall start with methods that might be feasible within the system as it is, but move towards radical solutions. Could groups increase their influence vis-à-vis government and each other by increasing the various factors, such as expertise and money, which allegedly lie behind bargaining strength? This is a realm in which some groups could make some headway. In a society professing to listen to rational argument the voice of the expert cannot be ignored, and any group is likely to gain in prestige and bargaining strength in so far as it can present accurate and relevant information grounded on the experience of its members. Alternatively, groups might increase their potential for disruption. The move towards direct acts and violence among some groups is a move to capitalise on their nuisance value. Such tactics will be eschewed by many reformers. The most extreme example of recent years has been the transition in the Irish Civil Rights movement from pleadings and marches to an out and out campaign of guerilla warfare, claiming hundreds of dead and millions of pounds worth of damage to property through bombings of factories and civilian targets. The campaign has reopened the question of a united Ireland, but otherwise it is too early to tell whether the underprivileged Catholic population will gain from it in the end. There was no quick pay-off from violence: it probably produced diminishing returns, particularly when 'defenceless' women and children became its victims.

In milder vein, the use of the strike as a disruptive tactic has enjoyed a certain success over recent years in Britain. In 1972 a miners' strike brought the country to conditions of shortage and blackout reminiscent of the war years and caused an initially contemptuous government to capitulate. A threat of a national strike 5 months later over issues arising out of the Industrial Relations Act again prompted what looked to most like governmental capitulation. Obviously there is nothing new about strikes, and the strike of post office workers in 1971 was for them a dismal failure—but the strikes of early 1972 were of a different character. They were more than strikes for higher wages; they were attempts to exert direct pressure on the government's policy and legislation by methods outside the negotiating table. Such tactics are, of course, barely feasible for the small campaigning group, though there are occasions when even they can wield the threat of violence effectively—the Stop the Tour campaign's threats to disrupt matches effectively prevented South African cricketers touring England. Of late, however, politicians and judges have shown themselves increasingly alarmed at this trend towards violence, which they believe, probably rightly, to be deprecated by the mass of the population. The severe sentences on members of the Angry Brigade, an anarchist subsection judged responsible for bomb attacks on politicians and political targets, testify that isolated violence will be contained by fierce and duly legal repression. Groups thinly spread over the country or comprising infirm or otherwise disadvantaged members would, of course, find such tactics impossible to sustain, even if they wanted to use them.

Other resources that allegedly improve a group's bargaining power are internal assets such as good organisation, leadership skills, political connections and money. It may be true that rich and powerful groups, like the captains of industry, have superior influence, or that groups with indispensable expertise will exercise authority. On the other hand it was possible in 1967 for the Abortion Law Reform Association, which had limited finances and, compared to the medical groups opposing it, few technical skills, to gain a dramatic success.

By contrast the campaigning record of the Voluntary Euthanasia Society makes depressing reading. Up until 1961 the history of the VES had been roughly equivalent to that of ALRA, but the disaster of the thalidomide babies gave that Society no help because it did not aim to introduce automatic mercy killing for this type of case, but only for cases in which it was the express wish of a dying patient. In the early 1960s, while ALRA was gathering strength, the VES continued its usual moderate programme of literature distribution and advertising. Then the tide began to flow in favour of the reformers. In 1966 membership reached 500, a figure ALRA had achieved only a couple of years earlier, and with a new chairman and secretary the VES programme became somewhat more vigorous, though it never reached the intensity of the ALRA programme, and the issue never gained the same popularity in the mass media. To some extent this may have been due to the problems of euthanasia, particularly that of guarding against the wilful murder of old people by their relatives (though it may be argued that this is no worse than destroying healthy babies for 'social' reasons). On the other hand the VES committee lacked the professionalism, verve and nerve of ALRA campaigners, and when its real chance came, in 1967, caution delayed it so long that it was overtaken by events.

From 1967 onwards VES worked on a Bill, and plans were under way to have it introduced into the Lords, but their supporters there felt that the Bill would stand a better chance if it had the blessing of the medical profession, and some time was spent trying to secure this, while the VES abstained from press comment so as not to rock the boat—in marked contrast to ALRA, which in its triumphal period was not in the least inhibited by such considerations. The delay proved wasteful for the VES, which had little hope of winning over the medical profession, and by 1969, when its Bill was introduced, it was too late. Paradoxically the very success of the abortion reformers operated to the disadvantage of the VES: it was said that the Medical Termination of Pregnancy Act had opened the door to abortion on demand and, quite apart from technical objections to the Euthanasia Bill, the peers were not going to make such a mistake again. The government, though in principle sympathetic, thought the Bill technically unworkable, and it was rejected. Public opinion, however, as shown by the polls, supported it.

It is easy to show that as a campaigning group ALRA had substantial advantages over VES. It was a better source of information; its membership, income and expenditure were two or three times as high; and its public campaign was altogether more courageous. It was extremely fortunate in receiving a wave of favourable publicity throughout the mass media, and, above all, it had increasing support among MPs. Similarly ALRA compares well with the Divorce Law Reform

Union and the National Campaign for the Abolition of Capital Punishment during the 1960s.

It was on much more even terms, however, with the Homosexual Law Reform Society, which was its equal in political connections and as a source of expert information, and whose campaign, revitalised in 1962 by its secretary, Antony Grey, was scarcely less vigorous. If ALRA had Kenneth Robinson and Douglas Houghton, the HLRS had Robinson and Leo Abse. Comparisons between other factors can be seen in tabular form.[3]

TABLE 3

	Inc (£)	Exp (£)	Supporters	Polls
ALRA	1853	1753	1000	36 social
				8 deformity
				61 rape
HLRS	5330	5186	1000	63

It seems that, if anything, the HLRS was rather stronger than ALRA, and might have been expected to make a bigger contribution to the Sexual Offences Act than in fact it did. But the characteristics of a group alone are insufficient to guarantee its successful intervention in the legislative process, its role being conditioned by a whole set of historical circumstances and by the personalities concerned with it. This is what makes accurate guidelines and prediction difficult. Certainly the ALRA campaign was well run and vigorous to a degree, but, as comparison with the HLRS shows, that cannot guarantee success. The answer lies elsewhere.

For many years before the thalidomide disaster the ALRA committee had been working with Glanville Williams, Professor of Jurisprudence, on the text of a Bill. In 1965, when Lord Silkin agreed to introduce the matter in the Lords, the medical profession and the churches had only just begun to formulate their views, and in the absence of any other authoritative definition of the subject Professor Williams' Bill became the ground on which other groups were forced to debate. By 1966 ALRA had established itself on a political scene in which many government ministers were known to be sympathetic to abortion law reform. In fact Home Office support encouraged David Steel, successful in the ballot, to introduce an abortion Bill. Simms and Hindell note that 'it was not until November 1966 that Steel first felt he understood the subject and began to know what he himself wanted in the bill'.[4] So ALRA, before the Bill was introduced, had been able to play a leading role in drafting it, and had further established itself as the background group doing clerical and lobbying work in its defence.

By contrast, when it came to the drafting of the Sexual Offences Bill, its basis was the Wolfenden Committee's Report. Although the HLRS pressed for more radical moves, and although the legislature in fact did not go as far as Wolfenden had recommended, Wolfenden guided the thinking of all parties. It provided precisely that statement of authority which was lacking in the abortion case. The successful campaign for homosexual law reform began with a motion introduced by Lord Arran in 1965; he was in contact with the HLRS but frequently acted off his own initiative, and was generally less susceptible to group guidance than Lord Silkin. Similarly, though Leo Abse, who introduced the ultimately successful Sexual Offences Bill, was a member of the HLRS executive, this did not give the Society any greater influence, since he had firm ideas on psycho-sexual development which, combined with his and Lord Arran's reading of the political situation, made him insist, for instance, on 18 as the stipulated age of adulthood, and oppose the Society on other matters.

Taking all points together we would infer that ALRA's ability to play a major role in the passage of the Medical Termination of Pregnancy Act can be attributed (1) to its

vigorous campaign and use of opinion polls, which set it apart
from weaker groups such as the Divorce Law Reform Union
or the Voluntary Euthanasia Society; (2) to the lack of any
authoritative statement on the issue; (3) to the readiness of
the Bill's sponsors to listen to ALRA's voice; and (4) to the
fact that the Abortion Bill was a private member's Bill, which
reduced the likelihood of government domination. We would
not claim that this combination of factors is the only recipe
for success, or even guarantee that it could work again, since
details must be different in every case; but at the most general
level the example indicates that groups are most successful
when parliamentarians are indecisive.

Another instance of successful pressure-group intervention
concerned commercial television. Pro-commercial interests
started, according to Wilson, with a good foothold within the
Conservative party in the House of Commons, and for 2 years
worked extremely hard to penetrate the minds of the Conservative leadership. They were assisted within the House by
a miscellany of subgroups opposed to the BBC's monopoly,
and outside it by the larger advertising agencies and equipment
manufacturers, who supplied at first advice and later a full-
blown publicity campaign. The hostile lobby, though emerging
rather on the late side, had distinguished extra-parliamentary
backing and sufficient support inside Westminster to convince
the government that it was necessary to curb the power potential of the advertisers by various devices, including a strong
Independent Television Authority. Without analysing this case
in any greater detail, we can suggest that the reason groups
were conspicuously active and able to achieve results in this
instance was because of the strong intra-parliamentary base
enjoyed by the commercial lobby. The fact that this lobby was
a subgroup within the Conservative Party then in power gave
them double access to Parliament and the centres of decision-
making. The fact that the government could not make up its

mind whether the second channel should or should not be commercial further strengthened the power of the lobbies, both for and against, and the fact that the Labour Party in opposition also offered no clear line, being divided on the issue, further strengthened the group's hand against the government. The commercial lobby was also able to threaten the minister with a revolt of Conservative backbenchers, aided by some support from the opposition benches, a situation analysed many years ago by Prof Finer as one in which groups have a good chance of success.[5] What was special about the TV example was that it was the product of an intra-parliamentary initiative. The brief period that elapsed between inception and Act, when compared to the prolonged struggles of the proponents of abortion, indicates the advantage of a parliamentary foothold.

The conclusion from these case studies is that groups can exert maximum influence when governments are indecisive or lack a policy but are not actively opposed to reform, and where the MPs most intimately involved are either closely allied to group interests, as in the case of commercial television or open to group suggestions, as with abortion. Obviously it would be difficult for groups to manufacture situations of this sort, and so their possibility of participation is always likely to be contingent upon variables largely beyond their control.

Despite this generally pessimistic conclusion, there may still be ways in which groups could enlarge their influence by playing the parliamentary system more effectively. At the moment one block seems to be the fact that they are given little importance by the legislators. An example from the USA may be illuminating.

A case study of some business legislators in the State legislature of Vermont suggested that senators fell into different categories: (1) the non-generalisers, who perceived every event as unique and failed to recognise consistent factors in group-

L

ings; (2) the faction-orientated, who interpreted events as part of a struggle between families competing for power; (3) the programme-orientated, who saw the session's work as a series of interlocking decisions; and (4) a number who saw events in terms of how they would affect group interests.[6] Most of the senators, therefore, simply did not conceptualise events in terms of group interests, though some thought groups important, and others that groups could only play a significant role when events were moving in their direction anyway. The group of non-generalisers tended to think of lobbying as highly immoral. The older, more experienced, more cosmopolitan senators were more likely to interpret events in a broader context of group interest.

The point is that legislators are human. To many of them the parliamentary world is central, and existence within it tends to shape their perceptions, highlighting intra-parliamentary moves and blurring the significance of external events and groupings. Obviously legislators are affected by pressure groups whether they recognise it or not, and indeed their hearty denial of it bodes ominously for democracy; but in so far as they repudiate being pressured, they appear to be defining groups as illegitimate influences, and changing this definition is not going to be easy.

A study in the USA by Lester Milrath suggests that legislators are most impressed not by groups but by constituency opinion.[7] The facts of the American electoral system may, of course, account for the legislators' feelings in this case, but it may still be a point relevant for British groups. Milrath suggests that groups should mobilise electoral opinion or show it to be in favour of reform, a technique certainly exploited by ALRA. He also suggests that there is no substitute for the personal approach and personal encounter between the legislator and group representative, and also stresses the value, confirmed by our own case studies of concentrating one's lobbying on key figures. The most striking example of this in the crop of British case studies is recorded by Hindell in his study of the Race Relations Bill, when he attributes the change of the Home Secretary's policy to lobbying by representatives of the Campaign against Racial Discrimination and in particular the influence these arguments had on one particular member of a cabinet committee.[8] To exploit tactics such as these, groups must have a sound working knowledge of who is who and what is what on the parliamentary scene.

Groups may be able to learn something useful from studying the efforts of successful earlier groups, but the fruits of such study are likely to be meagre so long as governments, MPs and peers regard groups with anything approaching distaste or distrust. If groups are to become more effective in their approaches to Parliament, their legitimacy must be improved. It is possible that the current lack of enthusiasm for groups stems from the very knowledge that only a few of them do approach Parliament, and that unequal endowment does give certain groups an initial advantage; this may be what legislators have in mind when receiving group overtures with caution.

Is there any possibility of increasing the participatory activity of the British public? Even the trade unions only cover half the British labour force, and we have seen that the membership of campaigning groups is extraordinarily small. The Abortion Law Reform Association claimed at peak only a couple of thousand members and the opposing Society for the Protection of the Unborn Child only a few hundred. The Conservation Society has notched up about 5,000 members in a few years and is still growing, though again the figure is miniscule if one considers that the whole population may be endangered by pollution. Mancur Olson has cynically remarked that the membership of such groups will inevitably be small because they offer few benefits to members.[9] Paying a subscription is like making a charitable donation, yielding no reward save moral satisfaction. Under present circumstances the reform will be neither hastened nor delayed by individual contributions, yet the non-contributors will, if the campaign is successful, profit equally with the contributors. This is the long-standing problem faced by trade unions, which negotiate wage increases that are enjoyed by unionist and non-unionist alike. Their solution has often been to enforce the closed shop, but such an expedient is hardly open to campaigning groups like ALRA or the HLRS.

However, even supposing that by extending their services rendered pressure groups did manage to recruit more massive memberships, this in no way guarantees the involvement of that membership. As we have seen, even the existing groups, which presumably recruited the hardiest devotees to a cause, were still organisations in which the bulk of members were passive subscribers. Must this be the inevitable fate of mass organisations? Writing on political parties in the 1930s, the Italian Roberto Michels coined the phrase 'the iron law of oligarchy' to describe the way in which parties that originate in mass fervour and democratic idealism gradually edge towards centralism and direction of the more passive many by the more active few.[10]

There must be many reasons why people fail to participate more actively in the organisations they belong to. One, of course, is the sheer number begging one to join them, with their welter of committees, subcommittees, working parties, meetings and demonstrations. Most people, however, are not even active in one organisation. Some who have tried it have found political experience disappointing and frustrating. The source of power always seems to be somewhere else and there always seem to be insuperable objections to one's self-evidently sensible suggestions. Many people dislike politicking, with its tightrope between fame and unpopularity. Others must feel that it involves moving into unfamiliar regions of lawyers and documents in which they would lack the necessary expertise and self-confidence. Anyway the demands of family life and the debilitating nature of the working day prevent most people from doing more.

In general it is easier to let other people do things for us because on most matters we have an enormous capacity for tolerance. It would be perhaps nice if working hours were shorter, or if vegetables cost less, but we do not feel that we can do much about it.

Maybe the tolerance we exhibit is a form of self-protection. In a complex world of multiple products, things to do, places to go, every activity involves so many decisions that if we had to think about all of them we would die from exhaustion. However, most of us are so far from reaching this limit that there is still scope for greater involvement. It may be handy for the individual not to have to decide what his factory shall produce—but someone is making that decision, and why should he? We let him because acceptance and obedience were fed into us at the teatable and the classroom desk when we bowed to the authority of our parents and teachers as to what the world is like and our inferior position within it. Contemporary education in the first and middle schools may be shaping a more involved self-directing adult, but it will obviously be several generations before pressure groups reap any benefits from this.

Given that the prospects for mass involvement are not immediately great, we shall for some time to come be left with something similar to the existing system. Maybe we have shown ways in which some groups may be able to enhance their performances, yet even if each group were operating at its optimum, the problem of domination by economic interests remains. The study of reforms of the code of sexual morals suggests a certain independence of the moral from the economic sphere, yet it cannot be doubted that in many matters economic influences are paramount. Jobs and the money earned by work become the flywheel of existence, and those who can put us out of work, or claim 'if you do this my industry will close', are powerful indeed. Thus we are unlikely to do anything to imperil our short-run standard of living and the 9 to 5 routine, and, in consequence, the malevolent, calculating and competitive habits which pervade all aspects of our existence.

On this basis Peter Buckman, in a stirring book entitled *The Limits of Protest,* has argued that the original purity of reformist ventures is inevitably sullied by a compromise with the social system as it is. He illustrates his point with reference to those poverty programmes in American cities, which started out as an attempt to redistribute the resources of the USA, but ended up with white capitalism and exploitation in the ghetto being replaced by black capitalism. The solution ameliorated the situation but left the fundamentals of the status quo undisturbed.

The case in point in contemporary Britain is conservation. Over the past 4-5 years there has been rapid growth of concern over pollution, conservation of the countryside, disposal of waste, population problems and food production. The secondary product of the materialist culture is a trail of despoliation, yet it is unlikely that the solution to the problem will be one that renounces materialism. The solution to the problem of atmospheric pollution will not be to reintroduce the horse and buggy but to build more expensive automobiles. Too much is contingent on industry for its needs not to be a a major consideration. Buckman's view is that only after a revolution which transforms the economic foundations will other reforms become possible.

There is a second argument which supports Buckman's conclusion. Earlier in this chapter we argued there was a strong case for increasing the role of interest groups. But how would the competing claims of different groups be reconciled? Since some groups would still be more numerous, richer or more skilled than others, struggles between them could never be equal. The capital punishment case is an ideal example. It is the liberal's nightmare. Suppose after all the mass of the British public had been successfully organised against abolition. As democrats we could not have denied them, yet the evidence of the experts had shown for 40 years that the death penalty was not a deterrent to murder. Reform of the law on homosexual practices undoubtedly meant an enormous amount to a few people living in shame and fear, yet the reform was held up in favour of the many more people who might be against it and yet had little to lose by it. How can one measure the relative claims of numbers against expertise, need against mass prejudice? How does one choose between doctors who don't want to perform abortions and women who want them?

It is a British misconception that there is a rational answer to every question and that reasonable men can in cognisance of 'the facts' reach reasonable decisions. This optimistic philosophy fails to observe that, even where people understand each other's difficulties and positions, real differences of interest and value can remain unreconciled, and so long as this is true it is necessary to produce some rule of thumb to choose between them, and no rule of thumb is other than arbitrary. We have tried to see which pressure groups are successful and why. We have suggested how, within the present system, groups may or may not be able to become more potent, yet in the end we come to wonder if groups are such a good thing after all. Proliferation of sectional interest solves nothing.

We have pictured factionalism as the war of all against all. Paul Wolff, in a critical essay on the pluralist conception of America,[11] implies that sectional conflicts are resolved by a cocoon of mutual tolerance, which means that major problems are sidestepped rather than solved. Are there alternatives to stalemate or mutual destruction? Wolff calls for a new spirit of community which would unite people in a national interest over and above their sectional interest, but, as he has noted earlier, people find it hard to identify with broad nebulous units. Are not our loyalties to family, friends and colleagues much dearer to us than our role as members of the European Economic Community? In any case, the call to a common humanity is an immorality in the face of a system where some through power and wealth are allowed to experience the humanity more fully than others. Only when real and salient differences of interest are eradicated can Wolff's spirit of community open its wings and flutter into the light.

Notes to this chapter are on p173

Notes and References

1 The Role of Pressure Groups

1 See, for instance, Punnett, Robert Malcolm. *British Government and Politics* (1968), or Birch, A. H. *The British System of Government* (1967)
2 Whitehouse, Mary. *Cleaning up TV* (1967)
3 For example, McKenzie, R. T. 'Parties, Pressure Groups and the British Political Process', *Political Quarterly* (1958), 1-27; Finer, Samuel. *The Anonymous Empire* (1958); Stewart, J. D. *British Pressure Groups* (1958); Potter, Allen. *Organised Groups in Modern British Politics* (1961)
4 See Beer, Samuel. *Modern British Politics* (1965); Moodie, Graeme & Studdert Kennedy, Gerald. *Opinions, Publics and Pressure Groups* (1969); Roberts, Geoffrey K. *Political Parties and Pressure Groups in Britain* (1970)
5 Walkland, S. A. *The Legislative Process in Great Britain* (1968)
6 For instance, Connolly, W. E. *The Bias of Pluralism* (New York 1969); Wolff, Paul. 'Beyond Tolerance' in Wolff, Paul, Moore, Barrington & Marcuse, Herbert. *A Critique of Pure Tolerance* (Boston 1965); Mills, C. Wright. *The Power Elite* (New York 1956); Miliband, R. *The State in Capitalist Society* (1969), esp Ch 6
7 Finer, Samuel, note 3 above; Eckstein, Harry Horace. *Pressure Group Politics* (1960), 33; Beer, Samuel, note 4 above, 320; Longley, L. D. 'Interest Group Interaction in a Legislative System', *Jnl Politics* 29 (1967); Moodie, G. & Studdert Kennedy, G. note 4 above, 64; Roberts, G. K., note 4 above, 135; Wootton, Graham. *Interest Groups* (1970), 83
8 McConnell, W. *Private Power in American Democracy*

2 The Years of Victory for the In-groups

1 For a readable account of changing ideologies of parties, electorate and pressure groups, see Beer, Samuel. *Modern British Politics* (1965)

M

2　Readers unfamiliar with the technical details of policy-making and the legislative process may find Walkland, S. A. *The Legislative Process in Great Britain* (1968) helpful background reading to this book.
3　Gorer, Geoffrey. *Exploring the English Character* (1955)
4　Gorer, Geoffrey. *Sex and Marriage in England Today* (1971)
5　An interesting historical account of the period is contained in Hopkins, Harry. *The New Look* (1960)
6　British Medical Association. *Report of Committee on Medical Aspects of Abortion* (July 1936); an account of the debate of 25 April 1936, p 230, and the report is reprinted in the *British Medical Journal*
7　*Report on an investigation into Maternal Mortality*, Cmd 5422 (April 1937)
8　For an account of the trial, see *British Medical Journal* (1938)
9　Ministry of Health & Home Office. *Interdepartmental Committee Report* (1939)
10　Simms, Madeleine & Hindell, Keith. *Abortion Law Reformed* (1971)
11　Hansard, Commons, Vol 511 (27 February 1953), Col 2506
12　Hansard, Lords, Vol 185 (26 January 1954), Col 411
13　Hansard, Commons (28 July 1955), written answer, Col 176
14　Hansard, Commons (26 January 1956), written answer, Col 47
15　Hansard, Commons, Vol 634 (10 February 1961), paras 853-91. Renton's speech for government is in paras 872-8
16　The second reading debate is in Hansard, Lords, Vol 161 (24 March 1949), Col 693
17　Hansard, Commons (16 February 1948)
18　Hansard, Commons, Vol 467, Col 2799
19　Hansard, Commons, Vol 466 (8 July 1949), Col 2501
20　Hansard, Commons, Vol 467 (20 July 1949) Col 1367
21　Hansard, Lords (23 November 1950)
22　Hansard, Commons, Vol 485 (9 March 1951), Col 926
23　*Royal Commission on Marriage and Divorce: minutes of evidence.* For an independent account of the Commons findings see McGregor, Oliver Ross. *Divorce in England* (1957)
24　*Royal Commission Evidence*, 146
25　*Royal Commission on Marriage and Divorce, Report* (1956)
26　*Minutes of Standing Committee* (6 March 1963)
27　Hansard, Commons, Vol 676 (3 May 1963), debate Col 1555; see esp Col 1562
28　Tuttle, Elizabeth. *The Crusade against Capital Punishment in Great Britain* (1961); also Christoph, J. B. *Capital Punishment* (1962)
29　Hansard, Commons, Vol 210 (1927), Col 2036
30　Calvert, Eric Roy. *Capital Punishment in the Twentieth Century* (1927)
31　Hansard, Commons (16 February 1928)
32　Hansard, Commons, Vol 233 (5 December 1928), Col 1220
33　Hansard, Commons, Vol 231, Col 241
34　*Report from the Select Committee on Capital Punishment* (1930)
35　Hansard, Commons, Vol 449 (14 April 1948), Col 979
36　Hansard, Lords, Vol 156 (1 June 1948), Col 19

37 Hansard, Lords, Vol 157 (20 July 1948), Col 1002
38 *Royal Commission on Capital Punishment, Evidence* (1949)
39 *Royal Commission on Capital Punishment, Report*, Cmd 8932 (1953)
40 Hansard, Commons, Vol 536 (10 February 1955), Col 2064
41 Much of our detailed evidence here comes from the Gardiner papers —a private collection of relevant letters and documents thoughtfully deposited at the British Museum by Lord Gardiner
42 Hansard, Commons, Vol 548 (16 February 1956), Col 2536; see esp Cols 2556 and 2655
43 Debate Hansard, Lords, Vol 198 (10 July 1956), Col 679

3 *The Organisation of the Rival Groups*

1 Reported in the *British Medical Journal* (30 May 1970)
2 Keleney, Stephen. Unpublished personal history of the Marriage Law Reform Society
3 Ibid

4 *In Which Pressure Groups Appear to Be Successful*

1 Polls by NOP and Gallup taken in the latter months of 1964 range between 65.3 per cent and 70 per cent in favour of retention
2 For a thorough and independent account of ALRA's activities and its contribution to the Medical Termination of Pregnancy Act, see Simms & Hindell. *Abortion Law Reformed* (1971)
3 Conducted by NOP
4 Church of England, Church Assembly Board for Social Responsibility. *Abortion: an Ethical Discussion* (1965)
5 See leader in *British Medical Journal* (29 January 1966)
6 Royal College of Obstetricians and Gynaecologists. *Legalised Abortion* (1966); see leader in *British Medical Journal* (2 April 1966)
7 *British Medical Journal* (November 1966)
8 Simms & Hindell. *Abortion Law Reformed*
9 Ibid, 177-8
10 See Hindell, Keith & Simms, Madeleine. 'How the Abortion Lobby worked', *Political Quarterly*, 30 (1968)
11 See *Minutes of Evidence, Royal Commission on Marriage and Divorce*
12 See *The Times* (6 May 1967). Lord Gardiner speaks to Marriage Guidance Council Annual Conference.

5 *Parliament's Role—What Influences It*

1 *Report of the Committee on Homosexual Offences and Prostitution*, Cmnd 247 (1957)
2 Sanderson, J. B. 'National Smoke Abatement Society and The Clean Air Act 1956', *Political Studies*, 9 (1961), 236-53

3 For independent histories of this struggle see Hyde, H. Montgomery. *The Other Love,* and Lord Arran in *Encounter* (1972)
4 Richards, P. *Parliament and Conscience* (1970), 149. This book provides an independent account of the passage of these and other Bills through Parliament
5 Simms & Hindell. *Abortion Law Reformed*
6 Richards, Peter. *Parliament and Conscience,* 177
7 Finer, Samuel Edward et al. *Backbench Opinion in the House of Commons* (Oxford 1961)
8 Richards, P. *Parliament and Conscience,* Ch 9, which is acknowledged as based on the work of Margaret Fuller
9 Derived from Marx, Karl. *The German Ideology* (1845-6)

6 *The Influence of Groups Reconsidered*

1 See submission of church groups to Royal Commission on Marriage and Divorce
2 See Richards, P. *Parliament and Conscience*
3 See, for instance, Reiche, Reimut. *Sexuality and the Class Struggle,* trans Bennett, Susan (1970), Ch 2; Reich, W. *The Sexual Revolution* (New York 1969); and Marcuse, Herbert. *Eros and Civilisation* (1968), and *One Dimensional Man* (1968), 70-2
4 See note 6 to Ch 1
5 Miliband

7 *From Particular to General*

1 Dowse Robert & Peel, John. 'The Politics of Birth Control', *Political Studies* (1965)
2 Driver, Christopher. *The Disarmers* (1964), and Parkin, Frank. *Middle-class Radicalism* (Manchester 1968)
3 Potter, Allen. 'The Equal Pay Campaign Committee', *Political Studies* (1957)
4 See in Moodie, G. & Studdert Kennedy, G. *Opinions, Publics and Pressure Groups* (1969)
5 Wilson, H. Hubert. *Pressure Group* (1961), 338-68
6 Sanderson, J. B. 'National Smoke Abatement Society and the Clean Air Act 1956', *Political Studies,* 9 (1961), 236-53
7 Steel, David. *No Entry* (1969)
8 Hindell, Keith. 'The Genesis of the Race Relations Bill', *Political Quarterly,* XXXVI (1965)
9 Richardson, J. 'The Making of the Restrictive Trade Practices Act,' *Parliamentary Affairs,* (1967), and *The Policy Making Process*
10 Barnett, Malcolm Joel. *The Politics of Legislation* (1969)
11 Richards, P. *Parliament and Conscience*
12 Eckstein, Harry Horace. *Pressure Group Politics* (1960)
13 Self, Peter & Storing, Herbert J. *The State and the Farmer* (1962);

also Pennock, J. R. 'Responsible Government, Separated Powers and Special Interests', *American Political Science Review*, LVI (1962)

14 Crossman, Richard. Text of Eleanor Rathbone lecture delivered at Sheffield University (May 1971)

15 Martin, L. W. 'The Market for Strategic Ideas in Britain', *American Political Sciences Review*, LVI (1962)

16 See note 11 to Ch 1

17 Sanderson, J. B., note 6 above

18 PEP. *Advisory Committees in British Government* (1960)

19 Stewart, J. D. *British Pressure Groups* (1958), Ch 1

20 PEP, note 18 above, 99

21 Self, Peter & Storing, H. J., note 13 above, Ch IX

22 Martin, L. W., note 15 above

23 Richardson, J., note 9 above

24 Hindell, Keith, note 8 above

25 Steel, David, note 7 above

26 Wilson, H. H., note 5 above

27 Stewart, J. D., note 19 above, 88

28 Barnett, M. J., note 10 above, Ch 8

29 Stewart, J. D., note 19 above, 60ff

30 Hindell, Keith, note 8 above

31 Wilson, H. H., note 5 above

32 Richardson, J., note 9 above

33 Barnett, M. J., note 10 above

34 Sanderson, J. B., note 6 above

35 Stewart, J. D., note 19 above, 96ff

36 Steel, David, note 7 above

8 *What of the Future?*

1 Lane, J. H. in Salisbury, Robert H. *Interest Group Politics in America* (New York 1970)

2 Bauer, Raymond Augustine *et al. American Business and Public Policy* (New York 1963)

3 Derived from material supplied by the societies

4 Simms & Hindell. *Abortion Law Reformed*, 176

5 Finer, Samuel. *Anonymous Empire*, 74

6 Garceau & Silverman in Salisbury, note 1 above

7 Milrath, Lester. *The Washington Lobbyists* (Chicago 1963)

8 Hindell, Keith, note 8 to Ch 7

9 Olson, Mancur. *The Logic of Collective Action* (1965)

10 Michels, Roberto. *Political Parties*, trans by Paul, E. & Paul, C. (1959)

11 Wolff, Paul, see note 6 to Ch 1

Appendix: The Progress of Reform

Date	General Events	Capital Punishment	Euthanasia	Abortion	Divorce	Homosexuality
1925		NCADP founded				
1929		Select Cttee				
1930		Sel Cttee Rpt				
1935			Found'g of VES	ALRA founded		
1936			Bill in Parl rejected			
1937					Herbert Act	
1938			Birkett Cttee Rpt			
1939	War years					
1945	Labour Govt elected					
1946	↑				Founding of MLRS	
1948		Criminal Justice Bill Royal Commission set up				
1951	↓		Parl Debate		Eirene White Bill Est of Royal Commission	
1952	Conservative Govt elected					
1953		Royal Commission reports	J. Reeves Bill			
1954						Wolfenden
1955		Founding of NCACP				
1956	Suez-Hungary				Royal Commission reports	
1957		Homicide Act				Wolfenden Report
1958						Founding of HLRS
1959	Conservative Govt re-elected					
1960			K. Robinson Bill			
1961					Leo Abse's Bill	Parl Debate
1962	Profumo scandal					
1964	Labour Govt elected					
1965		Murder Act ↓				
1967				Abortion Act ↓		Sexual Offences Act ↓
1969			Failure of Euthanasia Bill ↓		Divorce Act ↓	

Bibliography

This bibliography covers only some of the more significant sources. Further information is available from the author or from the various pressure groups.

ABORTION LAW REFORM

British Medical Association. *Report of Committee on Medical Aspects of Abortion* (1936)

British Medical Journal, passim.

Church Assembly Board for Social Responsibility. *Abortion* (1965)

Hindell, Keith & Simms, Madeleine. 'How the Abortion Lobby Worked', *Political Quarterly*, 39 (1968)

Interdepartmental Committee Report (Birkett Report 1939)

Jenkins, Alice. *Law for the Rich* (1960)

Report on an investigation into Maternal Mortality, Cmd 5422 (1937)

Simms, Madeleine & Hindell, Keith, *Abortion Law Reformed* (1971), which contains an excellent bibliography on wider aspects of abortion

St John Stevas, Norman. *The Right to Life* (1963)

BRITISH POLITICAL SYSTEM—HISTORICAL AND DESCRIPTIVE

Beer, Samuel. *Modern British Politics* (1965)

Birch, A. H. *Representative and Responsible Government* (1964), and *The British System of Government* (1967)

Miliband, Ralph. *The State in Capitalist Society* (1969)

Punnett, Robert Malcolm. *British Government and Politics* (1968)

Walkland, S. A. *The Legislative Process in Great Britain* (1968)

CAPITAL PUNISHMENT

Calvert, E. Roy. *Capital Punishment in the Twentieth Century* (1927) The original compendium of statistics

Christoph, J. B. *Capital Punishment* (1962)—especially good on period 1955-7, and contains a good bibliography

Gardiner papers—deposited in Manuscript Room, British Museum

Home Office Research Unit. *Murder*, pamphlet (1961). The Howard League for Penal Reform, 125 Kennington Park Rd, London, SE 11, can supply other pamphlets

Report from the Select Committee on Capital Punishment (1930)

Royal Commission on Capital Punishment, Evidence and Report (1953)

Sellin, Prof Thorsten. *Capital Punishment* (1967)

OTHER CASE STUDIES OF PRESSURE GROUPS (BRITAIN)

Barnett, Malcolm Joel. *The Politics of Legislation* (1969)

Dowse, Robert & Peel, John. 'The politics of Birth Control,' *Political Studies* (1965)

Driver, Christopher. *The Disarmers* (1964)

Eckstein, Harry H. *Pressure Group Politics* (1960)

Finer S. 'Transport Interests and the Roads Lobby', *Political Quarterly* (1958), and 'The political power of private capital', *Sociological Review* (1956)

Hindell, Keith. 'The Genesis of the Race Relations Bill', *Political Quarterly*, XXXVI (1965)

Lakey, George. 'Technique and Ethos in Non Violent Action', *Sociological Inquiry* (1968)

Martin, L. W. 'The Market for Strategic Ideas in Britain', in *Am Pol Sci Rev*, LVI (1962)

Pennock, J. R. 'Responsible Government Separated Powers and Special Interests', *Am Pol Sci Rev*, LVI (1962)

Potter, Allen. 'The Equal Pay Campaign Committee', *Political Studies* (1957)

Parkin, Frank. *Middle-class Radicalism* (Manchester 1968)

Richards, Peter. *Parliament and Conscience* (1970)

Richardson, J. *The Policy Making Process*

Sanderson, J. B. 'National Smoke Abatement Society and the Clean Air Act, 1956', *Political Studies* 9 (1961)

Self, Peter & Storing, Herbert J. *The State and the Farmer* (1962)

Strauss, George. 'Pressure Groups I have known', *Political Quarterly* (1958)

Whitehouse, Mary. *Cleaning Up TV* (1967)

Wilson, H. Hubert. *Pressure Group* (1961)

Wootton, Graham. 'Ex-servicemen in Politics', *Political Quarterly* (1958), and *The Politics of Influence*

DIVORCE

Church of England. *Putting Asunder* (1966)

Divorce Law Reform Union. Pamphlets are available from 39 Clabon Mews, London, SW 1

Herbert, Sir A. P. *The Ayes have it* (1937), an account of the passage of the 1937 Act

Latey, W. *The Tide of Divorce* (1970)

Law Commission. *The Field of Choice*, Cmd 3133 (1966)

McGregor, Oliver Ross. *Divorce in England* (1957)

Pollard, Robert. *The Problem of Divorce* (1958)

Royal Commission on Marriage and Divorce, Evidence and Report (1956)

EUTHANASIA LAW REFORM

Church Assembly Board for Social Responsibility. *Decisions about Life and Death* (1965) contains a wide bibliography
Downing, Arthur Benjamin. *Euthanasia and the Right to Death* (1969)
Exton, Smith, in *Lancet* (5 August 1961)
Hinton, John. *Dying* (1967)
Hughes, G. *Peace at Last* (1960)
Leak, K. 'Care of the Dying', *The Practitioner,* Vol 161 (1948)
The Voluntary Euthanasia Society, 13 Prince of Wales Terrace, London, W8, can supply further information.

HOMOSEXUAL LAW REFORM

Albany Trust, 32 Shaftesbury Avenue, London, W1, can supply a wide range of information
Arran, Lord, in *Encounter* (1972)
Grey, Antony & West, D. J. 'Homosexuals', *New Society* (27 March 1969)
Hyde, H. Montgomery. *The Other Love* (1970) contains a useful bibliography.
Schofield, Michael. *Sociological Aspects of Homosexuality* (1965)
West, D. J. *Homosexuality* (1960)
Westwood, Gordon. *A Minority* (1960)
Wildeblood, Peter. *Against the Law* (1958)

MORALS AND VALUES IN BRITAIN (general)

Gardiner, Gerald & Martin, Andrew. *Law Reform Now* (1963)
Gorer, Geoffrey. *Exploring the English Character* (1955), and *Sex and Marriage in Britain Today* (1971)
Hopkins, Harry. *The New Look* (1960), a historical account of the decades since World War II
Society of Friends. *Towards a Quaker View of Sex,* pamphlet (1962-3)
Williams, Glanville. *The Sanctity of Life and the Criminal Law* (1958)

POLITICAL THEORY AND PHILOSPHY (ESPECIALLY WITH A BEARING ON PRESSURE GROUPS)

Almond, G. A. 'Comparative Study of Interest Groups and the Political Process' in Eckstein H. & Apter, D. *Comparative Politics* (1963)
Buckman, Peter. *The Limits of Protest*
Castles, F. *Pressure Groups and Political Culture* (1967), and 'Business and Government', *Political Studies,* XVII (1967)
Key, V. O. *Politics, Parties and Pressure Groups* (1964)
Kornhauser, W. *The Politics of Mass Society* (1960)
Plamenatz, John. 'Electoral Studies and Democratic Theory', *Political Studies,* 6 (1951)
Truman, D. *The Governmental Process* (1951)
Wolff, Paul. 'Beyond Tolerance' in Wolff *et al. A Critique of Pure Tolerance* (Boston 1965)
Wootton, Graham. *Interest Groups* (1970)

PRESSURE GROUPS, POLITICAL SYSTEMS—FOREIGN

Bauer, Raymond Augustine *et al*. *American Business and Public Policy* (New York 1963)

Berle, A. A. *Power without Property* (USA 1959)

Blaisdell, D. C. *American Democracy under Pressure* (1957)

Erhmann, D. *Interest Groups on Four Continents* (1960)

Frye, G. 'Changing relations between parties and pressure groups in Germany', *World Politics* (1965)

Froman, R. 'Impact of Interest Groups in U.S.A.', *Am Pol Sci Rev* (1966)

Garceau, Oliver. *The Political Life of the American Medical Association* (1941)

Longley, L. D. 'Interest Group Interaction in a Legislative System', *Jnl Politics*, 29 (1967)

Merges, I. 'The role of business elites in Chile', *Jnl International Affairs* (1966)

Mills, C. Wright. *The Power Elite* (New York 1956), and *Causes of World War Three*

Salisbury, Robert H. (ed). *Interest Group Politics in America* (New York 1970)

Thornburn, D. 'Role of Business in Canadian Politics', *Can Jnl Econ & Political Science* (1964)

Truman, David. 'The American System in Crisis', *Political Science Quarterly* (1959)

PRESSURE GROUPS IN BRITAIN

Finer, Samuel. *The Anonymous Empire* (1958)

McKenzie, R. T. 'Parties, Pressure Groups and the British Political Process', *Political Quarterly* (1958)

Moodie, Graeme & Studdert Kennedy, Gerald, *Opinions, Publics and Pressure Groups* (1969)

Potter, Allen. *Organised Groups in Modern British Politics* (1958)

Roberts, Geoffrey. *Political Parties and Pressure Groups in Britain* (1970)

Stewart, J. D. *British Pressure Groups* (1958)

SOCIOLOGY OF SOCIAL MOVEMENTS

Blumer, H. in Lee A. *New Outline of the Principles of Sociology* (1946)

Cameron, William Bruce. *Modern Social Movements* (New York 1967)

Chapin, S. & Tsouderos, J. 'Formalisation Observed in Ten Voluntary Associations', *Social Forces* (1954-5)

Gusfield, J. R. *Protest, Reform and Revolt* (1970)

King, C. W. *Social Movements in the United States* (1956)

Messinger, S. L. 'Organisational Transformation', *Am Soc Rev* (1955)

Smelser, Neil J. *Collective Behaviour*

Turner, R. 'Collective Behaviour and Conflict', *Sociological Quarterly* (1964)

Zald, M. & Ash, R. 'Social Movement Organisations', *Social Forces*, XLIV (1966)

Index